MORAL FIBER

Character and Belief in Recent American Fiction

WESLEY A. KORT

FORTRESS PRESS   **Philadelphia**

For Phyllis

Library of Congress Cataloging in Publication Data

Kort, Wesley A.
  Moral fiber.

  Includes bibliographical references.
    1. American fiction—20th century—History and
criticism.   2. Religion in literature.   3. Characters
and characteristics in literature.   4. Literature and
morals.   I. Title.
PS374.R47K59   813'.54'09382   81–71389
ISBN 0–8006–1624–3   AACR2

9398L81   Printed in the United States of America   1–1624

Contents

Preface

An understanding of the relation of character in recent American fiction to religion requires an interpretive framework which, drawn from the literature and not imposed upon it, allows readers to relate texts both to one another and to religion in American culture. This book attempts to provide such a framework.

The attempt has required two contrary tasks. The first is analytical and systematic. This task takes the reader below the surfaces of narrative texts to the structures by which character has its place in the narrative form and by which character is shaped. The result of this task has been to propose a set or a system of beliefs as undergirding or enfolding the depiction of character in American fiction. The second task is cultural and historical. It takes the reader outward and backward in order to determine the religious importance and identity of this system of beliefs.

By undertaking both tasks, this book does not exhaust the possibilities of either. Its purpose is to clarify the relation of character in American fiction to religion and not to clarify narrative or religion in American culture in themselves. It is hoped that by being both synchronic and diachronic in method some justice has been done to the topic. The purpose of this study is to move forward, if only a small way, toward the goal of recognizing and substantiating the inextricable involvement with, even dependence upon one another, of religion and literature. It is hoped that the book will provide a common ground for specialists and laymen as well as for both students of religion and of literature to judge for themselves what advance has been made and how it could be increased.

The ideas and findings incorporated in this book were tested in public on several occasions, and I benefited from people who offered criticism and encouragement. I would like to thank Giles B. Gunn for his response to papers I presented at annual meetings of the American Academy of Religion. I am also grateful to Patricia Ward for inviting me to present a lecture at Pennsylvania State University and to J. Hillis Miller and Nelvin Vos for generously commenting on it. I was also aided by participants in the conference on religion and literature hosted by Duke University in 1977 and sponsored by the Lilly Foundation, for several of them, especially Edwin Cady, responded to my paper. Finally, I had the pleasure of presenting two lectures at Vassar College in the spring of 1980, and I profited from my conversations with faculty there, particularly with my host H. Patrick Sullivan.

I want to thank a number of people here at Duke University. I have benefited from the interest several graduate students have taken in this project: Ms. Diane Mowrey and Mr. William Jeffries from the Department of English; Mr. Robert Johnston from the Religion Department, who is now on the faculty at Western Kentucky University; and, especially, Ms. Amy-Jill Levine, whose editorial skills proved invaluable for the preparation of the manuscript. Professor David Rhodes, a visiting scholar during the academic year 1980–81, gave encouragement and helpful suggestions. I also wish to thank the administrators of the Cooperative Program in the Humanities, who awarded me a summer research grant in 1972 to begin this study, and of the Duke University Research Council, who gave me a similar grant in 1976. Finally, I have relied on the support and wisdom of several of my colleagues, especially Kalman Bland and Harry Partin.

Duke University   Wesley A. Kort

Introduction

Students of religion are never far from literary criticism. Since the major matters of religious traditions are conveyed in recognizable literary forms, especially narrative, the dependence of religion on literature and the study of religion on literary criticism cannot go unrecognized indefinitely.

Two questions arise: Why has narrative so commonly been asked by traditional communities to bear the burden of religious meaning? and, Do narratives written recently, in a society which does not think of itself as religious, continue to convey religious meaning? One answer will serve both questions: narratives in the past and today, in other cultures and in our own, convey religious meaning because of the elements by which narrative is constituted.

This answer counters assumptions which, although more easily taken, do not weather testing. One such assumption is that narratives have religious meaning when authors are religious or include religion in their works. While there is obvious validity to this position, it does not answer the questions because it deals only with some narratives or with work by certain authors; however, the answer given above does include all narratives.

Similar problems stem from the assumption that the relation of narrative to religion lies in the reading, particularly when religious or theologically trained people read narratives and begin commenting on their importance for religious life and thought. Again there is validity to this position, especially since literary theorists are becoming increasingly attentive to the aesthetics of reception and to the creative act of reading. But this position will fail us because the mutual involvement of narrative and religion derives from something accidental, the nature or interests of the reader.

The answer we have given, that narrative's relation to religion arises from the elements of narrative, not only opposes commonly and more easily held assumptions but also seems to deny obvious facts. One of these is that there is no such thing as narrative to which we can point, but there are countless narratives, as varied as are people—their experiences, their fancies, and their ways of communicating. People hear and tell stories all the time, from the nursery to the nursing home, from Chicago to China, from the first primordial campfire to last evening's cocktail party. Is it possible to pursue narrative as a single unity amidst all of this diversity and pluralism?

Recent narrative theory has been engaged in just such a task. Diversity is viewed as a surface matter. At one level, everyone has a story and everyone's story is unique; but at a deeper level, constants appear. These constants, often grouped under such headings as functions and actants, constitute a complex but finite set or system of possibilities. The term narrative, when used in the singular, refers not to surfaces but to a deep structure which can anticipate the many variables of narratives in the plural. In order to raise the question of narrative and religion, then, we should move neither to the author nor to the reader; we should move below the surface. The question before us is the relation of the elements of the narrative structure to religion.

Finally, the answer we have given seems to contradict what is obvious because, as anyone can see, narratives are constituted not by elements but by words. Again, this response has the advantage of undeniable validity: no words, no narrative. While it is true that narrative is speech, it is a certain kind of discourse; it stands out from language. We know when we are being told a story less because of the language being used than because of what the language serves, namely, the establishment of the elements of narrative. Narrative has a form, a structure which shapes the language.

The relation of narrative to religion, therefore, cannot be studied by moving from narratives to their authors or readers or by staying at their surface levels. We must posit a narrative system or structure, and we must see why and how religion is related to it.

It is possible to indicate the structure of narrative and still to avoid a new vocabulary or forbidding neologisms. The common critical terms—character, plot, atmosphere, and tone—will do.[1] A narrative requires actors (character), involved in processes (plot), under certain conditions (atmosphere), and with a relation to a teller (tone). The first two elements, character and plot, account for the dramatic potential in narrative; the remaining two, atmosphere and tone, account for narrative's lyrical potential. All four elements are required.

In a particular narrative, however, all four elements need not be of equal importance. In fact, one of the elements in the system will usually dominate the others and bend them toward itself,[2] or two of the elements will team up and shape the narrative at the expense of the other two. Consequently, variety is to be expected in the world of narrative as well as consistency. There are, and can be, character-dominated, plot-dominated, atmosphere-dominated, and tone-dominated narratives. The texts chosen for this study are character-dominated.

Now that we have pointed out the four corners of the narrative world, we can raise the question of the relation of this structure to religion. If we look at each of the elements, the relation will begin to become clear.

Atmosphere is the element which requires that boundaries be set in the world of a particular narrative. Although setting contributes greatly to atmosphere, boundaries involve more than time and place. In one narrative animals speak like people, while in another they do not. In this narrative characters fly to other planets, while in that one they are limited to earth. A wide separation may exist between what is possible in one narrative and what is possible in another. But in both, boundaries of some sort have been set and must be observed. This means that because of atmosphere, narratives raise and answer the question of what is possible. There is no answer to this question, of course, although there is a public consensus of some kind. But people vary greatly in what they believe to be possible, and some will entertain expectations in their lives which others reject out of hand. Atmosphere unavoidably relates narrative to belief because the questions of the boundaries, limitations, or conditions in and for human life are answered with belief. People also differ in their belief as to whether the boundaries or conditions of life are favorable to human well-being or indifferent or even hostile. The writer and reader of narratives, therefore, are involved with belief not by choice or training but because the element of atmosphere requires it.

This is also true of plot. Are the processes of which characters and events are a part destructive or beneficent? Are they inherently meaningful or meaningless? In one narrative characters find themselves in processes which are restorative, even redemptive. In another characters are crushed relentlessly by processes which are cruel or arbitrary and are reduced to shadows of their potential selves. People vary greatly in their beliefs concerning the temporality of human life, whether it is to be trusted or defied, whether it is part of a larger, meaningful whole or devoid of value. A narrative, by virtue of plot, is inextricably involved in belief because of the answers it implies concerning such questions, for all such answers have the status of beliefs.

Tone accounts for the presence of the teller in the tale, particularly the teller's attitude toward the material. This attitude has both physical and axiological dimensions. The teller is a participant in the story or the teller stands far from it. The teller also judges the material by ridicule or praise, by indifference or commitment, by condemnation or approval. Even though in contemporary narratives tellers frequently withhold judgment, their stand or attitude nonetheless implies evaluation or an attitude toward value.[3] A narrative is always somebody's or some community's, and we encounter in any narrative the values and, consequently, the beliefs of the teller, directly or indirectly, clearly or faintly.

We are now prepared by this discussion to see character, the subject of this study, as one in a set of four constituent elements in the structure of narrative, as related to the others, and as separable from them only in abstraction. As was true for the other elements, character cannot avoid belief because of the questions which must be answered. Are people basically mean or worthy? What is the greatest evil to which human nature is prone? Can a person find escape from the threats to well-being which surrounding evils pose? Narratives, especially those in which character is a dominant element, imply answers to questions such as these, questions concerning the moral and spiritual constitution of personal life. Since narratives, both fictional and historical, have in the past so commonly been engaged by the moral and spiritual problems and potentials of personal life, the tie between narrative and belief at the point of character may be, of the four possibilities, the least surprising.

We ought not to think of these four elements and the beliefs which correspond to them as constituting a list, even though we have presented them in that way. We must go on to say that the four elements and the four kinds of beliefs constitute a structure. As the elements guarantee a wholeness for the narrative, so the four beliefs, taken together, are sufficient to constitute a human world. Any ongoing life, individual or social, requires or presupposes answers to the questions we have posed in discussing the elements. Therefore, narrative—the deep structure underlying the narratives we hear and tell—corresponds to, or imitates (in Aristotle's meaning of the word), the structure of belief which undergirds a person's or a people's world.

A study of belief in narrative can be carried on more fruitfully in relation to fictional than to historical narrative. This is because fictional narrative allows for more play with the structure of belief.[4] In fictional narrative events and characters can be subjected to beliefs, for example, while in historical narrative beliefs must submit to the characters and events. Fictional narrative, in addition, directs attention away from immediate references, leads to "impertinence" in order to create a new pertinence.[5] This delayed effect can reveal something about ourselves or our world which usually is hidden or has been sensed only faintly before. Fictional narrative has more freedom to turn attention to belief, and its semantic direction leads to realities or possibilities which lie below the surface or on the horizons of our worlds.

This study of fictional characters and their dependence on belief presupposes that characters are formed by two contrary sets of material. One theorist describes them by using a very helpful metaphor.

> The actor is first an empty ledger on the top of which is written only a proper name. As the narrative progresses, this empty ledger is progressively filled up with the entries . . . implied in the functions, and the personage is progressively created. . . .[6]

Although this metaphor sets the two components of character in clear contrast, it fails to suggest the shaping authority and the content of the stable component. The contraries in the element of character here referred to as ledger and entries correspond to the distinction in formalist theory between paradigmatic and syntagmatic components.[7] "Paradigm" suggests more contribution from the stable component, a shaping authority. This study of character rests on the conclusion that the stable aspect in the element of character is a belief concerning human nature which shapes the varying functions and qualities of personal life.

The beliefs which shape character range between ethical and ontological or moral and spiritual poles. When the moral or ethical pole is more important, we see characters as "good guys" and "bad guys." Moral traces are always present, even if the beliefs move far to the other side, the ontological or spiritual. Here the threats or evils have less to do with moral stature than with well-being, self-actualization, or personal existence itself.

These beliefs are concerned both with evil, whether moral or ontological, and with escape from, or overcoming of, the evil. The belief which shapes a character in a narrative, then, is an answer to a complex question: What is the greatest evil for or in personal life, and how can that evil be avoided or overcome?

This study of character is organized by the conclusion, based on an analysis of many texts, that there are three prominent answers to this question, three major beliefs which shape characters in recent American fiction. The first belief is that human nature is vulnerable to imprisonment within a world which human beings make and control themselves. Such imprisonment is an evil because it cuts off a person or a society from the natural sources of life. For this belief, nature is not something to be endured or even admired; rather, nature yields moral and spiritual fruits, while separation from it distorts and deprives personal existence. New life, even moral regeneration, is to be found in relationship with nature. For the second belief the greatest evil in human life is conflict, particularly the split between conflicting values. These values generally enter a person's life because of the influence of differing cultures. Cultural conflict easily leads to a sense of life as tragic and at war with itself. Deliverance from this evil takes the form of interpretation, a resolution achieved without the expense of one or more of the conflicting values. The third belief which shapes character in American fiction is that daily life represents an evil because of its incoherence and incompleteness. This threat must be met by transcendent possibilities or realities. Characters shaped by this belief do not turn to nature for authentication or resolution; nor do they negotiate cultural conflicts to heal their moral or spiritual quandaries. Rather, they seek a spiritual alternative or extension of ordinary life, a world elsewhere, believed in or imagined.

For the purposes of this study, American writers have been brought together into three groups depending on which of these beliefs shapes characters in their work. Furthermore, the general role of each belief in American culture is suggested. Following that, the religious importance of the beliefs is established by a study of their place in the work of representative American theologians and students of religion.

In the Conclusion to this study a further step is taken. A proposal is made that the three beliefs treated in the body of the book are not mutually exclusive but form a system. Together they constitute a complete image of what a person is or ought to be. This hypothesis leads, at the very end, to the question of the nature, source, and religious standing of this system of belief. As answer to these questions, the possibility is held out that these beliefs have an integrity and a tradition of their own.

An emphasis on that which contemporary writers share not only with one another but also with the tradition unavoidably slights the ways in which they differ. Attention to deep structure also tends to slight individuality and originality. Our intention is not, however, reductivistic. Rather, slighting of this kind is a price which must be paid for turning attention to the ways in which American fictional characters are shaped by beliefs and to the religious standing of those beliefs.

The study will slight matters of plot, tone, and atmosphere in the fiction studied because character is the focus of attention. In addition, one side of character will be emphasized, that which is constant and grants continuity. Consequently, we shall be more attentive to the overall shape of character depictions than to details of characterization, more attentive to what makes characters alike than to what makes them unique.

PART ONE

THE TERRITORY AHEAD

1

Confinement and Release

The belief concerning human nature which unifies the texts brought
together in this part of the book construes the principal threat to
human life as confinement within a humanly controlled world. Such
a world, closed in upon itself, is unstimulating, unnourishing, and
imprisoning. Delivery from it takes the form of escape or release.
Since it is a humanly controlled environment which incarcerates the
person, deliverance is achieved through contact with diverse realities
which can be grouped together as "natural." Escape or release, however, will be difficult because a humanly controlled world grants
security. Society, while confining, is also reassuring; in contrast, nature, while freeing, involves risk. Escape or release also becomes
difficult if the humanly controlled world is so pervasive and forceful
that the character dependent upon it loses the opportunity or ability
to move toward another environment. Concerning this issue, Richard
Poirier notes this major distinction in American narratives: in some
the search for an alternative environment is rewarded, while in
others the humanly controlled world overpowers "any effort of the
imagination to transcend it."[1]

This belief has an important place in American culture. We shall
examine some of its general characteristics and then discuss its role
in major texts in the narrative tradition and in the religious anthropologies of representative American theologians.

Release or escape from confinement usually means, for Americans,
going backward in time. The natural world is imaged as something
in the past, rejected or neglected, always there but, for the time of
imprisonment, increasingly unattainable. The move outward, then,

is often a return; "the territory ahead," says Wright Morris, "lies behind us, safe as the gold at Fort Knox."[2] In addition, release or escape to the natural world often means rejecting the corporate in favor of the individual dimension of the self. Therefore, persons with less than full enfranchisement within the society—members of racial or religious minorities, children, and, at times, women—find it more possible than do white, adult, Protestant males to renew contact with neglected natural resources.

Orientation to the past and to desocialization compels a Freudian critic like Leslie Fiedler to see this pattern of movement expressed in American fictional characters as regressive, even neurotic. The movement backward is for him a rejection of the complexities of adult life in favor of the innocence and simplicities of youth.[3] While this regressive factor may be present, the move to a simpler and more natural life is not in itself a simple or natural task; the move is fraught with uncertainty for the individual and with revolutionary, anarchical implications for the society which is rejected. A move toward the natural world increases the value of psychic energies which the process of socialization has forced the individual to modify or repress. Spontaneity replaces calculation; control and distinction-making are replaced by immersion in the energies and patterns of the preconscious life.

Critics such as Richard Poirier and Tony Tanner see the move to the natural as a quest for a natural style.

> The new American style was meant to release hitherto unexperienced dimensions of the self into space where it would encounter none of the antagonistic social systems which stifle it in the more enclosed and cultivated spaces of England and of English books, the spaces from which Lawrence escaped to the American West.[4]

This emphasis on a natural style is particularly important for the creation of characters who are also the narrators of their stories; natural language is a part of a more natural style of life.

It is not surprising that characters shaped by this understanding should appear in American literature. The evaluation of the contrary relation of society to the development of personal potential, the vast natural resources available to the American imagination, and the opportunity to develop a life free from the accumulated weight of European culture and history contribute to this anthropology. As

Henry Nash Smith states, ". . . the negative doctrine that civilization is wicked and the positive doctrine that untouched nature is a source of strength, truth, and virtue—occur sporadically in writing about the Wild West far into the nineteenth century."[5] Civilization is pernicious because "it interposes a veil of artificiality between the individual and the natural objects of experience."[6] Even though the orientation of the American imagination to nature was pressured by the steady domestication of natural environments and by our remarkable fascination for technological and economic power, the image of new life as a natural potential awaiting discovery continued as a safety valve, "an imaginative construction which masked poverty and industrial strife with the pleasing suggestion that a beneficent nature stronger than any human agency, the ancient resource of Americans, the power that had made the country rich and great, would solve the new problem of industrialism."[7]

Even today Americans are sustained by the belief that undergirding or surrounding us is a natural goodness, a resource able to provide an alternative to the confines of a humanly created world, able to revive and restore the undernourished or fatigued human spirit. Individual preoccupation with nature, youth, and the pre- or unconscious world seems undiminished.

Characters formed by this first belief concerning human nature can readily be found in our tradition. Three major texts in the canon of American fiction illustrate this: *Moby Dick, Adventures of Huckleberry Finn,* and *The Sun Also Rises.*

In Herman Melville's *Moby Dick* the transition made by Ishmael from society to the sea seems to be undergirded by an experience he had as a young boy. Confined to his room by his stepmother, after an extended period of privation, Ishmael felt a hand mysteriously touch his own.[8] The relation of the adult Ishmael to society and then his relation to the sea follow this exchange of deprivation for fulfillment, of a stepmother for a true mother. Going to sea is a substitute for "pistol and ball" not only because it is risky but also because shore-bound existence is deadly.

Leaving land for the half-known, frightening sea has a corresponding internal action, the move from a secure to a truer self. The sea corresponds to the uncertainties of the inner life: ". . . so in the soul of man there lies one insular Tahiti, full of peace and joy, but encompassed by all the horrors of the half-known life."[9] (chapter 57). The reader is led to these depths or extremities by means of a steppingstone progression.[10] Nantucket is already rather far out. The *Pequod* takes us further. We are involved in the voyage because the *Pequod* is a concentration of humanity and human potential; personalities are represented (the responsible Starbuck, the escapist Stubb, and the reductionist Flask), as are racial and cultural types. The *Pequod* is also foremost among whalers: her captain and crew know more about the sea, sailing, and whales than any others that they meet and, by implication, any others afloat. Early encounters with whales and other adventures experienced by Ishmael and the crew are further steppingstones to the encounter with Moby Dick.

The meeting with the white whale is the culmination of the process by which Ishmael moves from the confinement of society to the rebirth at sea. Moby Dick is constitutive to this culmination because he epitomizes all that is powerful, uncontrollable, and fascinating about the natural world; he does so because he lives in the sea, is a member of the sea's largest species, is the largest, most resourceful, and most respected member of his species, and is white. The attributes of deity associated with him are not intended as a case for pantheism; rather, it appears that Moby Dick is the most able creature in all the natural world to epitomize what is fascinating and intimidating, beautiful and terrifying, fulfilling and destructive in nature. By virute of his ambiguously meaningful power, Moby Dick is an objective correlative to the most profound of human capacities, able to create in those adequately endowed and prepared a uniquely complex response. The culminating event, then, prepared for negatively by shore experiences and positively by the experiences at sea, is a meeting between the best that man can muster—man's full emotional and intellectual capacities—and the best the sea has to offer—concentrated power and mystery.[11]

Ishmael is a rather ordinary person, someone like us. His spiritual experiences are marked by integration, dependence, and reflection. He is more oriented to the mothers, as shown in the Grand Armada scene, than to the fathers, and he is enclosed by a larger world. In contrast to Ishmael is Ahab—an obsessive and extraordinary person, oriented to the fathers and bent on breaking through the limits of the world.[12] Both characters are necessary to the story; together, ordinary and extraordinary, they constitute two kinds of responses to the mysterious immensities which lie around us in the natural world, powers and mysteries by which we are tested, corrected, and revitalized. Despite their differences, however, Ishmael and Ahab both reveal an impatience with shore life, with life in the humanly controlled world. Either forced to the natural by the unnatural or drawn to the natural obsessively by its power to possess the spirit, human life requires contact with nature. By that contact it is challenged and nourished, reborn or culminated.

The move from society to nature, from confinement to freedom and newness of life, is also central to Mark Twain's *Adventures of Huckleberry Finn*; but a different emphasis is found here. Rather than the capacity of nature, in its immensity and profundity, to sound the depths of human response and to invigorate the deepest levels of the spirit, this text emphasizes the development, in contact with nature, of a natural, human style, which, because it is natural, is also truthful, even moral.

Huck indirectly tells us about the way in which he has learned to speak naturally and truthfully. Chiefly, he avoids other ways of speaking and acting, because artificial, imitated, or deliberate styles are untrue. The person of integrity is not a construct but a natural product. Huck opens the account by committing himself to telling the truth, and the story itself concerns the way in which he was enabled to do so. If he changes at all, he develops increasing confidence in his truthful and natural style.

This move toward a natural moral style is marked by Huck's successful escape from imprisonments. He almost allows himself to be entrapped by the very contrary worlds of the widow and Pap; he becomes comfortable and secure in the style each offers. When he flees, Huck takes something of both with him: the charity of the widow without the social conformity, and the hedonism of Pap without the dereliction. The influence of the widow and of Pap can be seen in life on the raft.

A third style is represented by Tom's penchant for romantic fantasies. What Huck takes from Tom is the sense of life as a perilous adventure; without Tom's influence he would be more passive. What Huck avoids is Tom's tendency to distort human life in order to fit it more perfectly into imaginary models. Huck's natural, moral style assumes that human life can be pleasurable, charitable, and open to adventure.

The role of Jim in Huck's development is too complex to handle adequately here. The painfully unfortunate social position in which he stands ties Jim more closely to the natural world. This results in his great strengths: generosity, fidelity, and sincerity. But while Huck receives much from Jim and while their friendship is an important component of natural and moral life, Huck must maneuver around the complexities, sophistication, and deceptions of a social world in which Jim has little part. Despite his stature in the work, then, Jim should be seen as a character subordinated to the disciplining of Huck toward a natural, human style.

A major factor in Huck's development is the river. Rather than accept Richard Chase's suggestion that the river is a symbol of deity,[13] we should hold that the river is mainly the river but that floating down it is symbolic. Nor are the towns symbols of evil, in contrast to the paradisiacal river; rather, entering and leaving them is symbolic. Thus, emphasis should not be shifted from Huck to a contrast between civilization and the river. Huck's style allows him to maneuver past the hazards he encounters both on the river and in the towns.

The river contributes more, however; telling a good story, having a natural style, is like floating downstream. "I went right along," Huck tells us as he describes his style, "not fixing up any particular plan, but just trusting Providence to put the right words in my mouth when the time come; for I'd noticed that Providence always did put the right words in my mouth, if I left it alone."[14] Because his style is natural and moral, it is also subversive of social pretensions. This force is contrasted to other antisocial styles which are destructive. For example, the King and the Duke, although attractive to Huck because he had read a bit about royalty, play on the prurient instincts and the craving for titillation of the local populations. The antisocial attitudes of Emmeline Grangerford are oriented toward death. Huck's subversiveness implies moral ends and the enhancement of life.

Nature in *Moby Dick* is terrible and sublime; in *Huckleberry Finn* it comes to expression in a kind of human style supported by the natural flow of the river. In Ernest Hemingway's *The Sun Also Rises* natural resources which grant renewed life are far more internal, even psychological. The journey Jake Barnes completes is toward a new sense of rootedness in himself.

The three parts of his career resemble the three parts of Dante's *Divine Comedy*. Jake moves from the bleak and disorienting world of Paris, through the highly ritualistic purgatorial period centered in and around Pamplona, to the Paradiso of his newly found internal freedom and peace of mind in the last, brief section.

That Jake, like Dante, has reached a crisis midway through his life is made clear by Cohn's remark in chapter two: "Do you realize you've lived nearly half the time you have to live already?"[15] It is also suggested by the consequences of his injury. His state is one of rootlessness which is both physical, because of the loss of his sexual organ, and psychological, because of his lack of a spiritual center. Although Count Mippipopolous grants the respite from distress that his classical counterparts provide Dante in the *Inferno*, Jake's time in Paris is one of dislocation and frustration. The pilgrimage to Pamplona has as its purpose the correction of that state.

The second part of Jake's secular, self-determined way toward wholeness begins with Bill—a kind of Virgil who helps him part of the way—and with other pilgrims—a whole train of them from Dayton. These pilgrims are fellow Catholics, although Jake does not feel comfortable with them. The rituals performed during this part of Jake's pilgrimage suggest rootedness. Fishing, for example, grants a sense of location. In chapter twelve Bill uses the occasion to lecture Jake on the hazards of deracination: "Nobody that ever left their own country ever wrote anything worth printing. Not even in the newspapers." "You're an expatriate. You've lost touch with the soil," he says.[16] Bill is helpful, but he is too uncomplicated, too healthy.

Jake, however, cannot move from Bill to Christian rituals as Dante moved from Virgil to Beatrice. Although he tries to enter Christian institutions and practices and although he feels "a little ashamed" because he was all of the time "thinking of myself" while praying, Jake cannot dissolve his personal pilgrimage into these larger structures of communal and traditional acts. Even the feast of San Fermin and the bullfights do not fully embrace him. He betrays the code of the special group of *aficionados* by failing to keep

Romero pure, and the festivals of Pamplona are finally only a means toward his more individual and improvised healing. Yet, the major moments of ritual in this part—along with minor ones such as eating, drinking, dancing, bull-running, bathing, and the funeral—have productive results for Jake. He seems less distressed and insensitive to people than do the others.

It is fitting that, at the opening of the third part, Jake and Bill say their friendly farewells. Jake is now on his own. As he swims he seems at peace, floating on the water and diving deeply. Although reminded of his condition by the sight of a couple on the raft and although forced to rescue Brett, he comes through quite well. In the process he has achieved self-sufficiency, personal solidarity, and moral stature. He is not tempted from these realities by the fantasy of regretted, unattainable possibilities; he realizes that the relationship with Brett, in any case, would not have been good.

The role of nature in these three narratives is not identical, but in each of them the character finds natural resources which heal diseases caused by entrapment within a humanly made world. Such characters are also found in contemporary American narratives. William Styron's fiction is centered on the capacity of nature to overthrow the culture that represses it. Styron renders Southern in opposition to Northern settings, darker-skinned against lighter-skinned people, swamps against gas stations; in his fiction repression results in violent eruption. In Susan Sontag's novels we are given characters who, caught up in society's tendency toward abstraction, find their natural, internal lives alien and forbidding. Joseph Heller's characters are, it seems, wholly entrapped by a humanly made world which is destroying them. *A Separate Peace, Deliverance*—the list could go on.

The common attribute of texts in this first group is that they share a belief concerning what threatens or limits the person and how that threat can be overcome. According to this belief, the chief evil of human life is imprisonment in a humanly made world and the consequent isolation from that natural context by which one needs to be corrected, increased, and refreshed. This evil can be overcome by escape from confinement accomplished by renewed contact with natural aspects of human life or with nature. Despite the great differences between Melville and Mailer, Twain and

Oates, or Hemingway and Gardner, they share a belief concerning the moral and spiritual well-being of personal life.

This belief is not limited to literary texts. American religious thought tends, as does American literature, to be concerned with the position and well-being of the individual. Human evils and their corresponding cures are perceived in a similar way. We have in our culture, it seems, both a common preoccupation with the individual and a set of three controlling paradigms.

For example, the major and influential text by William James *The Varieties of Religious Experience* argues that the individual deeply needs relatedness of both an ontological and psychological kind. Ontologically, a sense of being at home in the universe is required; psychologically, continuity between the conscious and subconscious lives is needed. James writes, *"Religion thus makes easy and felicitous what in any case is necessary;* and if it be the only agency that can accomplish this result, its vital importance as a human faculty stands vindicated beyond dispute."[17] Religion is able to create a sense of unity with the world, and through religious conversion a person can experience a new continuity with the subconscious extension of his conscious life. James's famous discussion of conversion is largely determined by his estimation that, with whatever else may occur in experiences of this kind, resources of the subconscious life are making themselves felt, often suddenly, in the conscious self. He proposes the hypothesis that "whatever it may be on its *farther* side, the 'more' with which in religious experience we feel ourselves connected is on its *hither* side the subconscious continuation of our conscious life."[18] If our lives are indeed invaded by an unseen reality, this invasion takes place through the subliminal door.[19] The fruit of religion is, thus, a rootedness in the universe and a relation of the conscious to the subconscious.[20]

The focus of James's study is the individual person; he has little appreciation for the ecclesiastical or theological structures of religious communities. He works from an estimate of an individual's needs—not in a theocentric way, from the reality of God back to the consequences of that reality for human life.[21] His religious anthropology calls for an orientation not primarily to what is above but to what is below us, the universe of which we are a part and the subconscious continuation of our conscious lives. A basic, subliminal rapport with, or a being at home in, the universe, openness to the subconscious self, and a sense of acting meaningfully in the world characterize his belief concerning the moral and spiritual life of the individual.

Henry Nelson Wieman's religious anthropology directs attention to a natural power which transforms human life. He calls this force creative interchange, the creative event, or God. It transforms human life by releasing the person from the confinement of an already created value. The ·products of previous creative events have the potential of making people dependent upon them, thereby separating individuals from the possibility of ever new creative moments. One of the conditions for a creative event, then, is openness to others and to the world of which each person is a part. For Wieman, an example of this pattern can be found in the experience of the disciples with Jesus. The life of Jesus had been a creative event, but the disciples were tempted to be confined by it. Somehow a new event broke in which transformed their orientation to one another, to other people, and to their larger world. Wieman views the past as a potential prison because it has a demonstrated value which tends to obscure the need for future creative events. Such blockage is destructive for the actualization of human potential.

It is not inaccurate to say that for Wieman this actualization of value, the work of God, is a natural event.[22] A transforming power releases the person from the past and moves him to values quite beyond his expectations. The creative event produces a structure of relationships which is beyond intention; it undercuts and alters the previous arrangements of human expectation and desire.[23]

Bernard E. Meland adds a major note to this first paradigm because of his orientation to cultural anthropology. His principal concern is to address spiritual life in terms of those ways by which the individual is formed in primary relations to others and to his environment.

Meland finds fault with the religious anthropology of liberal Protestantism because it elevates individual consciousness "as the source and center of spiritual meaning and value."[24] He identifies this isolation and elevation of the rational self as the arrogance and "hardening" of sin, a refusal to recognize the primacy of "the relational aspect of man's existence and the depth of meaning" upon which conscious life depends.[25]

The guidelines he follows for his corrective to liberal religious anthropology are emphases on depth, on emergence, and on the categories of myth or intuition. "Depth" affirms the creative work of God in ordinary human affairs. "Emergence" suggests Meland's stress upon history, for depth is not primarily under us but behind us in the form of the richly meaningful resources accumulated by prior human attitudes and actions. "Myth" refers to an undergirding of conscious life by a preconscious structure in communities and in individuals, a meaningfulness which is felt, for example, when an occasion suddenly brings tears to our eyes. A person or a community should respond in faith, openness, and gratitude to these tacit resources and structures upon which a sense of meaningfulness depends.

A recognition of God, for which culture can prepare us, involves an appreciation for that persuasive and recreative force of love, forgiveness, and healing which Meland, echoing Whitehead, calls the "tenderness of life." God's work is primarily to be seen as melting the barriers which arise between people and which keep them from an awareness of their relation both to one another and to the prereflective meaning by which they are formed. The work of God, this good which is not of our own making, "transmutes sheer process into qualitative attainment."[26] It delivers us from evil, from a state by which, because of our anxiety, pride, or other distortion, we isolate ourselves from that creative force.

James, Wieman, and Meland see the soteriological process as an overcoming of confinement within a conscious or humanly controlled world, a confinement which results in alienation from forces or processes which lie below or behind human life. Evil is, or results from, an overevaluation of, and a dependence upon, the world of human consciousness and control. The good, psychological, natural, or cultural resources are always there; and isolation or encapsulation within a world limited to consciousness should yield to a reintegration of the individual or community with these forces. But reintegration is not easily achieved, for the move means risks, takes faith, and results in unpredictable changes.

The first kind of belief concerning human nature forms a spiritual tradition in America affecting both our literature and our religious reflection. It defines human evil as confinement within a humanly controlled world cut off from the natural and creative resources in psychic, cosmic, and cultural life. This evil arises from a person's preference for the security that a fixed, familiar, humanly controlled world can provide and a corresponding distrust of realities which lie beyond control. This destructive, evil state is not readily overcome, but if it is, then the walls of a world that has become a prison will be broken. Life moves to configurations which grant a deeper sense of belonging to a larger, natural reality by which the individual is maintained, corrected, and spiritually revived.

2

Norman Mailer and the Push Toward Experience

A consistent belief concerning the human problem and its solution underlies the corpus of Norman Mailer's writing and gives his characters their distinctive shapes. The category that most aptly indicates this belief is "experience." Although the character may distrust what he does not know and be tempted to prefer the comfort of a humanly controlled world, he encounters life only in and through experience.

Mailer believes that people in American society tend to cling to the comfort of what already had been done or made. They stamp out the unfamiliar and the future by imposing upon them past accomplishments. They predict, control, and limit what will happen; consequently, nothing new can occur. Americans live off the past instead of looking toward their future. Collectively as well as individually they prefer the tried to the true, the packaged to the raw, the fabricated to the natural. This self-protection depletes rather than preserves human life. Mailer's term for the resulting psychic or spiritual condition is "cancer."

Reinforcing this aversion to experience is a second characteristic of American life, the primacy of consciousness. The contemporary person, according to Mailer, elevates mind above emotions and circumstances. This process creates a condition which Mailer calls "schizophrenia." Since the mind can acknowledge and handle only a part of what can be encountered in the world, the rejected or repressed facts and forces are compelled to go underground. This unrecognized sewerage constitutes a subterranean river which distresses conscious life, divides the people against aspects of their world, and erupts either in individual acts of violence or in such corporate compensations as the vast and irrational violence Mailer refers to as "Vietnam."

Another way of describing the roots of the moral and spiritual diseases, cancer and schizophrenia, is to say that people lack confidence in the continuity between what is required for the enlargement of life and the potential in the world to grant what they need. People tend to distrust what they have not themselves domesticated. What lies beyond reach is often ignored, resisted, or caricatured. Thinking that the unknown territory ahead is evil, they fail to recognize that evil is actually the tyranny of the familiar, the repetition of the already tried, and the fear of exposure. Evil results from dependence upon a world which grants security, imprisons, and separates the individual from what actually is good, from creative contact with the untried, the uncontrolled, the new. And every moment, every act or word, has that kind of moral and spiritual importance. There is in Mailer's work a call to choose: life or death, good or evil, God or the devil.

Experience is the fresh, expectant, and sharply sensed encounter with the future and with what cannot be subjected to anticipation or to established patterns. A lively response to the unique in each particular experience arises from trust in the new—trust rewarded by sanity, freedom, and growth.

It is on the basis of experience that we can make the distinction among the characters which is indicated by the title of Mailer's first novel, *The Naked and the Dead.* As Stanley tells Croft, these men are all in for "an experience." Moving onto an enemy-held island with no reliable information about what lies ahead, they are in the very position that defines experience. The many who are incapable of it are dead.

Chief of the dead is General Cummings. He avoids experience by putting himself in front of maps rather than circumstances. He lives from his head down, and, as he tells Hearn, he turns life into a chess game. People like Wilson, Gallagher, and Brown avoid circumstances by fleeing into memories and fantasies centered particularly on their wives and other women. Sergeant Croft avoids experiences by resenting circumstances. He flails at them and so is unaware of any actual encounter with the terrain or with his men. Hearn, the liberal, can also be assigned to this group. He is indecisive and dependent; his acts of protest and disruption are merely irritants to others and stimulants to himself. Rationalists, dreamers, cynics, and liberals are numbered among the dead because they reject, or are incapable of, experience.

The group of the naked is small. Perhaps only Goldstein and Ridges are exposed and responsive to their circumstances, to things, to events, and to people around them. This is particularly clear in their relation to Wilson; Goldstein responds to his physical, Ridges to his spiritual, requirements. They do this, it seems, because they are well schooled in exposure. For Goldstein, Jewishness means a developed capacity for suffering, a long history of confrontation with circumstances. Ridges grew up on an economically low-yielding farm: "Storms were a basic part of his life; he had come to fear them, to bear with them, and finally to expect them."[1] Both men are religious; for Mailer's purposes this means primarily that both are aware of mystery, of the importance of what lies beyond control. They are sensitive to the world around them, unafraid of risks, alone, the naked among the dead.

When Mailer's characters are set in the America of the fifties, a change occurs. No longer does he stress a distinction between individuals according to their attitude toward circumstances. Basic to his second and third novels is the belief that American society is evil, dominated by fear, and dedicated to the eradication of the conditions for experience. Moral and spiritual health appear only minimally. Individuals must resist their surroundings if they are to establish themselves on a ground from which experience might arise.

In *Barbary Shore*, Michael Lovett moves in a world so opposed to human wholeness and health that he can survive only by writing. A victim of amnesia, he lacks personal roots in reality and, like the other inhabitants of the boardinghouse in which he resides, he lives in fantasies. An atmosphere close to apocalyptic pervades the work: Mrs. Guinevere, a Jehovah's Witness, predicts famines, wars, and plagues; Lonnie Madison paints her entire room, including the windows, black; and McLeod insists on the inevitability of global war and the replacement of human life with machines. In such an environment it is understandable that Lovett's novel depicts society as a large and confining institution from which people must escape to find a more promising day.

Like Lovett, Sergius O'Shaugnessy in *The Deer Park* writes in order to survive. Desert D'Or, California does not provide conditions conducive to experience. The setting, marked by repression, is a society of affluent conformity imposed on the site of a former mining community. The people are absorbed by the movie industry, and the movie industry devours human life. Teppis, president of Supreme Pictures, buys lives for productions. Others, like Marion Faye, trade in sex rather than experience it. Sergius has additional problems with his environment because during the war he lost the attitude of abstraction and impersonality and began to associate bombing with burning bodies. This association turns him against flesh and renders him impotent. Aggravating the life of Desert D'Or are the anti-Communist investigations of the Subversive Committee, a group which epitomizes the society's tendency to call every challenge, every hint of the new or strange, Communist. The Committee is itself schizophrenic, and its real interest is to seek gratification for its own sensual cravings. The conditions under which people live do not nourish; rather, they are actively engaged in preventing experience.

In *Advertisements for Myself*, Mailer elaborates his view of the human situation. Two powers which affect us are operating in the world. One promotes sterility, repression, conformity, and arrogance of mind; the other leads to growth, individuality, and instinct. All human actions contribute either to God's domain or to the devil's. If we do not recognize the need to fight against the devil, if we fail to choose, we contribute to his realm. The society is conditioned to serve in that direction. Eleanor and Sam, in "The Man Who Studied Yoga," for example, are caught between desire and action, between a revulsion for society and a fear of chaos. Suspended and indecisive, they avoid life by trying to avoid risk and pain. Yet, orientation toward experience means taking a stance against a society dedicated to expunging the very conditions that would make experience possible. Consequently, Mailer welcomes all antisocial impulses and causes: nihilists, criminals, addicts, restless minorities, and psychopaths. "The White Negro" is his call for an all-out struggle against the forces of evil.

Mailer's sketch of the larger spiritual situation in which human life participates reveals the resemblance of his work to that of the theologians previously mentioned, especially to that of Henry Nelson Wieman. In Mailer's theology God is a cosmic life-force who attempts to actualize his potential in time. To do this he must fight against the devil. In the battle God is directly helped or hindered by what people do. Every word or act performed in honesty and clarity is both a contribution to God's cause and a blow against the devil, against what is produced with "science, factology, and committee rather than with sex, birth, heart, flesh, creation . . ."[2]

Mailer's vivid delineation of the struggle for control of the individual's spirit leads him naturally to forms of power in society, particularly to political clout. Since the consequences of political influence are far ranging, and since the style of political leadership affects the attitudes of ordinary people, figures like the President must be given a sense of mystery and be taught to risk uncertainty for the sake of life. *Presidential Papers*, directed to John Kennedy, argues that the principal task of our national leader is to direct people away from hypocrisy, innocence, and the pursuit of psychic and physical security toward an awareness of the complications and ambiguities of their world. For example, Americans must be encouraged not to regard the alien as a threat; they should avoid labeling ideas and movements foreign to them as "Communist." The President can lead the people away from the drift toward cancer and schizophrenia—from the "sickening of our substance, an electrification of our nerves, a deterioration of desire, and apathy about the future, a defectation of the present, an amnesia of the past"—toward the risks and potential growth of a life open to mystery.[3]

Although Mailer's call to a fight for life sounds violent and even destructive, it is really the enemy that is violent. This deadliness often goes unnoticed by its real and potential victims. For example, in *Cannibals and Christians* Mailer contends that American architecture is a violent force, interchangeable and monotonous. The reigning style represses the "spirit of honest adventure and open inquiry which developed across the centuries from primitive man to the Renaissance. . . ."[4] It is a style that does not arise from a confrontation with what is naturally there; the terrain is leveled and the planned, prefabricated, multi-use unit is imposed upon it. The natural place contributes nothing. The signs of wrestling with its uniqueness are not to be found in the resulting structure. Creativity arises only in a fresh struggle with otherness; "whenever the environment resists, the result is a form."[5] But to repress and ignore the contrary and the actual is to enslave and destroy the imagination, to deny that position where "whatever created us wishes us to be, out to where it was conceived we would move."[6] The prisons in which we languish are locked from within by our own hands.

The principal characters of Mailer's next two novels try to escape those prisons. Steve Rojack, who narrates *An American Dream*, had what Mailer calls an experience; during the war he charged a hill in Italy and destroyed a machine gun nest. But rather than live toward new experiences, Rojack has made the deadly mistake of living off his past action. He trades the recognition he received for political, social, and financial security. Early in the narrative, tempted by the moon to jump from a balcony, he realizes that he has imprisoned himself and that the conditions of his present life threaten his capacity for growth.

Rojack's way of breaking out of the enclosure, the murder of his wife, is not a simple deed. Deborah, although possibly a victim of cancer, was alive to mystery and, at least to a degree, responsible for the potential for change in Rojack. Rojack values women because they are naturally more intuitive and because they are more capable of suffering than are men. Consequently, he derives much from Deborah and, later, from Cherry.

Kelly epitomizes one way of life which stands contrary to that which Rojack seeks. For example, his use of power fosters schizophrenia. Kelly wants Rojack to attend Deborah's funeral in order to pretend in public that everything is under control. Rojack tries to develop an ability to live before the unknown, between society and the gods. He does this principally by walking the parapet of the balcony. But even though he is able to risk confrontation with uncertainty, he flees at the end. This flight suggests that American society is unable to provide a place for a man on the mend to stand.

Disc jockey Randall Jethroe, the eighteen-year-old Texan narrator of *Why Are We In Vietnam?* reveals the quality of the American illness primarily by describing a hunting expedition to Alaska he made with his father, Rusty. His father wants a trophy, something to bring home that would prove his success, and he subordinates everything else to that goal. Heavily armed and led by guides, the hunters even employ a helicopter to locate game and "do the job." But most shocking to D. J. is Rusty's willingness to damage their relationship for the sake of success; he allows others to think that he, and not D. J., killed the bear. This act clarifies for D. J., Rusty's role as an executive of a plastics corporation as well as his competitive, exploitative, and repressive habits.

The trip to Alaska, however, also produces an experience for D. J. He and his friend Tex go up Brooks Range, leaving their weapons behind. There they confront someone else's world, the horror and beauty of nature, dangerous as well as gentle animal life. They stand in awe under the sublimity and vast silence of the aurora borealis.

Within these two novels we can detect subtle changes in Mailer's anthropology that are secured in *Armies of the Night*. There appears, first of all, a shift away from fighting the devil—in order to make available the conditions required for experience—to fighting the evil of society—such fighting being itself an experience. Second, there is a move from preoccupation with group warfare to battle as an increasingly individual act. In *Armies of the Night* Mailer rejects the group dimension of the struggle and becomes an army of one.

The Pentagon is an apt enemy for Mailer because it symbolizes so well the nature and use of power in America. Amorphous and impersonal, the Pentagon avoids accountability and fosters schizophrenia and cancer. The march has promise, however, particularly because those engaged in it did not know what to expect; ". . . politics had again become mysterious."[7] But this potential for meaning is undermined by Mailer's alienation from the liberals in the group.

Liberals err primarily by thinking that conflict can be removed from life. They view it as a temporary irritant, and they look forward to a "social machine of the future in which all irrational human conflict would be resolved. . . ."[8] For Mailer, life without conflict is plastic, static, and diffused. Paul Goodman, for example, even wants to take conflict and guilt out of sex, but without them, as far as Mailer is concerned, sex is a "superhighway to your own soul's entropy. . . ."[9] Conflict is integral to life, and the desire to avoid it grows out of a timidity toward living, out of an atrophied moral and spiritual vitality. Every act, including writing, is conflict-ridden, and without struggle there can be no growth or creativity.

Mailer's distance from organized and spontaneous political movements is clarified in *Miami and the Siege of Chicago*. The political parties and the mobs in the street constitute two destructive responses to the problem that society has become for the processes of individual growth and health. Neither totalitarianism nor nihilism will cure cancer. As the hotels of Chicago and Miami ignore or repress the stockyards or the swamps, the political parties are dedicated to the self-protective domination of real life. The nihilists react to this situation not in the name of life and growth but of death and destruction. In *St. George and the Godfather*, Mailer finds no improvement or new support in the political moods of the seventies. McGovern is a liberal, and Nixon secures his position by identifying himself with the mediocre and the inert. An interesting instance of political style is what Mailer calls the "Jeannette Weiss Principle," the use of an individual to satisfy the needs of diverse groups for recognition, "like double and triple scores in Scrabble. . . ."[10] The style compounds confusion, erases real distinctions, and throws a facade of unity over actual sources of creative difference.

NASA's flight to the moon attracted Mailer's interest not only because of the power the act required and the sexual imagery which it suggests, but primarily because of its potential to be the great adventure of the century, a move to uncertainty and a confrontation with mystery. But in *Of A Fire On the Moon*, he concludes that the possibilities for experience were removed from the outset by the reigning technological mind. The principal purpose seems not creative but competitive—to beat the Russians—and not expansive but repressive—to intimidate the irrationality and protests of American youth and minorities. The technological mind renders the astronauts interchangeable like the buildings; their language, euphemistic and indirect, suppresses emotion and individuality. Although the size of the rocket, the power of corporate will, and the sophistication of the technological mind are all very impressive, Mailer sees in the enterprise the arrogance of intellect and the inherent schizophrenia to which the society has fallen victim. He concludes that nobody actually went to the moon. Like tourists who go to a foreign country only to stay in a Hilton or Holiday Inn, Americans went to the moon housed within the familiar plastic veneer of their calculations and preconceptions.

Since Mailer increased his investment in the battle for life as an individual enterprise, it is understandable that he would take an interest in the women's liberation movement. His negative reaction to it arises from his anthropology. It is a strong reaction because, for Mailer, sexuality provides a crucial moment in the struggle that leads to life. In fact, a sexual metaphor is implicit in his understanding of experience.

Mailer detects in the movement a tendency to divorce people from their sexuality. This abstraction from bodily identity is, as we have seen, a clear symptom of our culture's illness. It means, finally, the subjection of the individual to a rationalistic and technological tyranny. Central to *Prisoner of Sex* is Mailer's evaluation of the struggle with "the other," and the other is most clearly to be found in a person of the opposite sex. Throughout his work it seems that the struggle waged in order to create new life, the struggle that gives rise to style, is a lover's quarrel. Therefore, the erasure of sexual distinctions threatens to destroy one of the few remaining arenas for experience. Another threat to this major focus is the mechanization of sex, its subjection to control. Preoccupation with techniques and the use of birth control devices limit the potential for experience. In addition, the movement is uncritical toward, even supportive of, society's tendency to attack the potential for life and growth that lies in the struggles and fulfillments of sexual relations. We are and must be, according to Mailer, prisoners of our sex, and it is only in full accord with our bodies that the transcendence—which in other places he refers to as the "Apocalyptic Orgasm"—can be granted. Sex is the central moment in which a person finds himself freed to a situation beyond his control in which individuality is transcended by the unifying and fulfilling growth-moment of orgasm.

The boxing ring, along with the bed, provides a concentrated instance of the lovers' quarrel which lies at the heart of creative struggle. The principal direction taken by Mailer in *The Fight* is less toward the interdependence of the combatants, however, than toward the powers which lie below and behind them, powers of which they are themselves manifestations. The Ali-Foreman fight in Zaire provided Mailer with the opportunity to depict personal power as strength derived from a fecundity that lies somehow under or behind the individual. The force, the dark richness of life out of which individuality arises, is epitomized in these fighters. The individual is a form of vital power which clarifies itself in a struggle with an opponent.

Most of the beliefs about personal life which constitute Mailer's anthropology can be found in *The Executioner's Song*. Gary Gilmore, American society, and the relation between these two—particularly in and through the legal and prison system—give Mailer fruitful ground to explore and affirm his beliefs. He does this primarily through the metaphor of clarity and the virtue of honesty.

These characteristics of the work join its two parts: the depiction of Gilmore's life from the time he was released from prison in 1976 to his execution nine months later and the description of the way the story was gathered. Gilmore's interest in clarity and honesty and the search of the reporters and writers, especially of Lawrence Schiller, both for insight into Gilmore's actions and motives and for accuracy in reporting them, join the man and his biographers, the life and the text.

For Gilmore and Nicole Baker, his girlfriend, clarity or honesty is opposed to what they call "bullshit." Their style and the value they place on it make them honest with one another and with their interviewers. The criterion of clarity distinguishes the prison from the mental hospital. In the prison the lines are drawn and things are clear; in the mental hospital patients act like guards and work with the doctors. Clarity and honesty also inform Gilmore's insistence that he be executed. He has committed the murders, and since the state has decided to kill him, the state should follow through on its decision.

The work of the writers—gathering details, sequences, and a sense of relationships—is nonexploitative because of the respect which the honesty of the principal characters elicits. Gilmore and Nicole are not defensive about or embarrassed by their actions, attitudes, or emotions. This does not mean that they lack a sense of privacy or propriety. But because personal areas are not artificially protected, the limits which the inquiry should respect, while tacit, have integrity.

It is fitting that the interviewers and Gilmore form a comradeship in the closing hours of his life. They do so primarily because of their mutual respect, but they also establish a clearing in the larger context of American indecisiveness, self-protective ambiguity, and evasion. The larger world of the reporting industry, of the legal system, and of such groups as the American Civil Liberties Union is incapable of expressing its convictions, of acting upon them, and of facing the consequences of those actions. The context is reactive and derivative. The group in the clearing has achieved a hard-won island of honesty in a system of large deceptions.

The stress on clarity not only forms a common characteristic in Gilmore's style and in the methods of the reporters, but it also constitutes a moral or human value which elevates those in the clearing above the context. This is the most provocative element in the work. Gilmore is guilty of two murders; he coerces Nicole into attempting suicide; and he seems to be drawn to pederasty. Nicole is sexually promiscuous, somewhat masochistic, and, at times, an indifferent mother. But their quality of honesty and quest for clarity grant them moral value.

For Mailer, honesty is a health, a discipline to truth, and a position with a creative future. The achievement of the novel lies in his ability to disclose the power and attraction of the virtue without mitigating the ambiguities and destructive propensities in Gilmore's personality and actions. Given the larger context of Mailer's writing, however, it is possible to say that the state and the society are more deadly in their repression and fear of honesty, in their own form of irresponsibility and destruction, than Gilmore. The killing of people by people, however horrible, is a human act to which we can eventually respond. But the killing of people by means of attitudes and habits characteristic of the society is inhuman or counter-human; it leads not to a fuller understanding of our humanity but to a loss of it, even to the loss of our capacity to understand it.

We can see in Mailer's large and varied corpus a consistent anthropology. The category of experience, defined as "any occasion where your senses are aroused beyond your control of them,"[11] indicates the positive element in his work. The negative element arises in response to a society which is dedicated to the gradual destruction of the conditions for experience. His characters find themselves within the unnatural, the fabricated, and the humanly controlled. To be delivered from this evil they must not succumb to the fear of risking the new. When they allow natural power to rise within them, they are open to creative challenges. Mailer's characters are shaped by the belief that human evil is confinement and that deliverance from evil requires interaction with natural resources. Such interaction leads to truthfulness and newness of life.

3

Joyce Carol Oates and the Inverse of Negative Relations

Like the other writers discussed in this section, Joyce Carol Oates creates characters whose lives are distorted because they have become unnatural. The cause of distress is estrangement from a natural substructure of interpersonal relationships. Oates reveals, through her use of character, not only what Americans are or might become. She uses shadow characters who pursue reduced, desperate, or painful relationships to suggest as well an inverse possibility: how important to self-actualization sound natural relationships are, and how characters come to realize this importance when faced with the loss or absence of such relationships. Her characters reveal dependence on primary relationships, on what Bernard Meland calls "the tenderness of life."

For Oates, characters are less important than the relationships between them. In *With Shuddering Fall*, Karen Herz's relations with her father and with her lover, the racing driver Shar, are characterized by the image of sacrifice. From the story of Abraham and Isaac at the beginning, through Karen's domination by her father, the use Shar makes of her and his rituallike sacrifice in the auto race, to the Mass at the end—the subjection of individual life to the desire for relationships is central.

The interest Karen and Shar have in self-sacrifice is unfortunate because both have suffered emotional deprivations. Both are dedicated to a process of self-purgation and passivity in order to experience the acceptance which they failed to receive in their respective families. Karen's background creates in her the ability and desire to perpetrate what she has suffered on others. She is well schooled in the power which withdrawal can exert, and she uses it in her relation to Shar. He, in turn, needs to push himself to the limit. The attraction between Karen and Shar arises from their compatible, complementary neuroses.

Clara Walpole in *A Garden of Earthly Delights* also perpetuates in adult life patterns of human relationship learned as a child. She is raised as the daughter of a migrant worker forced to leave his Kentucky farm during the Depression to find employment. Clara's family became an economic unit, an instrument of employment. Despite her varied career and sundry relationships, Clara does not change this tendency to convert human relations into economic or monetary ones.

Like other characters in Oates' novels, Clara experiences terribly reduced human relationships while expecting an almost religious fulfillment from her contacts with others. When she has sexual intercourse with Lowry she imagines the force lowering itself into her body to be God.[1] Also like other characters in Oates's fiction, Clara conveys her attitudes to her son. Particularly, she wants him to be someone "who would control not just isolated moments in his life but his entire life, and who would not just control his own life but other lives as well."[2] Armed with this attitude, her son gradually gains a controlling position in his stepfather's home. But the subjection of human relationships to some larger economic plan proves to be destructive. Her son thinks only in terms of manipulation and control, grows paranoid, and kills both his stepfather and himself.

In the last part of the novel, the aged Clara, watching television in a nursing home, likes violent shows best: "the dying gasps of evil men were only a certain familiar rhythm away from the opening blasts of the commercials, which changed only gradually over the years."[3] The tie between violence and the commercials is neatly made. As her father had been pulled from the land and reduced with his family to an economic unit, so Clara subjects life to economic and commercial considerations. She lives out the image of life forced upon her.

The title *Expensive People* suggests characters who also have become economic units or who subject their relations with others to monetary designs. However, the principal reason in this book for the evaporation of natural and nourishing human relations is not money but the vampire of imagination. Although Richard Everett's mother gives herself both to lovers and to social connections, she ignores her son primarily for the sake of her career as a writer. Richard's father is characterized by his position as a manager of various firms that manufacture wiring for weapons, a position from which he will prove himself "the sort of man who cannot bear to be outdone at anything."[4] The absence of his parents, the hole where they ought to be, does not leave Richard indifferent to primary relationships; rather, he is obsessed with them. We can infer that natural or healthy relationships are not objects of explicit or conscious concern. When such relationships are unavailable they become obsessively important for the person deprived of them. Their primacy and worth can be recognized in their absence.

Richard's position in relation to his parents is rather well depicted in one of his mother's stories, "The Molesters." The little girl in the tale becomes vulnerable to a molester because, unlike her parents, he notices her. Richard is impressed with the amount of understanding his mother reveals for the position of this child, but he concludes that "the sympathy she showed in her stories must have used up all the sympathy she had in her."[5] Having spent her emotion on imaginary children rather than on her own, she has deprived her son of her presence. "Mothers," he says, "who are always backing out of the driveway draw every drop of love out of us."[6] Concerning his father, Richard notes, "In my reading I came across Freud's remark that everyone's notion of God is based upon his unconscious notion of his father. Well, I am stuck with a sadistic, happy, back-slapping God and to hell with that."[7] It is not surprising that through acts of violence he should throw himself before his parents in order to be noticed. In addition to expressing anger and seeking recognition, Richard, in his violence, is trying to break through the darkness of his situation to where there is light.[8]

The setting of *them* lies at the opposite end of the social range from that of *Expensive People;* rather than in the suburb of Fernwood, the novel is placed in the slums of Detroit. The people incarcerated there have no available alternative environment, suffer the consequences of poverty in their interpersonal relations, and respond to their situations with desperation and violence. Life in the streets, alleys, and tenement houses is oriented to survival, welfare, borrowing or stealing, and prostitution. This orientation creates a sharp separation between actual existence and fantasy life. Jules, one of Loretta Wendall's children, often thinks of a different place, of open country in Michigan or California, of the future, or of some unexpected gift of money. At the end of the book he heads for California. Maureen, the daughter, stimulates her fantasy life with library books, and the world of novels is more real to her than her own. Both she and Jules regard money as being able to deliver them; money has a clear, clean force. Determined by conditions over which they have no control, these characters tend to be passive and resigned. Unprotected, they are vulnerable to rapid and drastic shifts of circumstance and to use and abuse by others.

Among the factors contributing to the degradation and distortion of human relationships, the most important in this book is the setting at the bottom of a humanly created world. Even the parks of the city are not natural but planned. As Jules walks along he sees a small vestige of natural life, some weeds in a vacant lot, and he is struck by the fact that these weeds are not there by human design. Because they live in the absence of natural life, Jules and Maureen live unnaturally. The inner city, a violent place because it is unnatural, offers no support for the growth of human relationships or for the actualization of personal potential.

The distresses that mark personal life in America are, for Oates, not only caused by suburban and urban settings. They are also caused by fundamental attitudes. *Wonderland*, one of two novels dealing with the elite professions, renders the destructive orientation to others of Jesse Hart, a man who rises from the least promising of social origins—he is the only survivor of the murder of his family by his father—to one of society's most prestigious positions, neurosurgeon. The trauma and the success are related: Jesse, who must repress the memory of his family, pursues medical training as a discipline of abstraction above the circumstances of particular human lives. The medical people in this book are asocial and ahistorical. As a result, the adult Jesse's relation to others is not very different from the violent disconnections perpetrated by his own father.

Jesse's tutor and patron is Dr. Pedersen, who imparts to him a faith in design. The human power to abstract grants a person control: ". . . I am able to make a map of my life that will be mine, while other people bump into one another in stupid crowds and herds, like animals."[9] Rationality offers protection against, and an alternative to, what Pederson calls "the terrible darknesses and odors of reality, the terrible silence of the universe that does not know our human language."[10] Bizarre products of this dissociation from reality are Pedersen's two children: his daughter, a mathematical genius in an unbelievably obese body from which she feels separated; and his son, who has almost translated himself into a musical score.

The training Jesse receives at medical school, in the second of the book's three parts, fortifies his ascendancy over reality. "Human beings fear mechanisms," one instructor tells the class, "because they do not understand that they are mechanisms themselves."[11] And Jesse's friend Dr. Monk remarks, "We in medicine should go after the ultimate cure—the separation of the spirit from the flesh. Everything else is unsanitary nonsense."[12]

The violence of these attitudes is detected by the female characters: Jesse's mother, Helda, his wife, Helene, and Mrs. Pedersen. Helene calls Dr. Perrault—who thinks that personality is an illusion or tradition that dies hard—a killer, and she feels that Jesse is destroying her. Occasionally even Jesse seems not wholly convinced of these notions and attitudes; he has a difficult time remaining aloof from the patients in the emergency room, and he senses that some word ought to be spoken into the silence of his relationship with Helene.

The principal consequence of Jesse's attitude is his daughter's escape into a fringe community headed by a man who dominates her completely. She is vulnerable to this kind of "family" because of the deficiencies in her father's relationship with her. Although his pursuit of his daughter as well as his many trying experiences affect him deeply, Jesse is incapable of changing his orientation. Both he and the society seem to acknowledge no attitude toward other people except the violent one assumed and epitomized by the medical profession in general and by surgeons in particular.

Wonderland, then, diagnoses a basic illness which, according to Oates, is caused by recoil from the human and natural, from one's own body and from relations to other people. But no prescription for cure seems offered by the novel. This may be the darkest of Oates's fictions, but the inverse of these negative relations can, of course, be inferred. Medical science merely epitomizes a general, social valuation of abstraction, and life is defined by the process of growing alienation. Natural relations would constitute the inverse of these unnatural ones: a grounding of individuality in bodily existence and sympathetic mutuality, in what Bernard Meland calls "the tenderness of life."

While medical science undermines human relations by strategies of alienation, the legal profession distorts them by removing the common ground from which they grow and by defining them as abstracted and adversary. The role of this profession in society and its effects on human relations is central to *Do With Me What You Will*.

Oates describes the American legal system as unnatural. This situation is aggravated by the general separation of society from nature. Characters who encounter nature for the first time are surprised by it. "If you could see this part of the world, how beautiful it is! It is like the edge of the world here, the clean mountains and rocks and the sky, not like Pittsburgh."[13] The two splits reinforce one another —society and its legal system against nature and personal relations— and characters seem to be required to choose between them. Elena has trouble making the choice because she is passive. As a woman in a male-dominated world and as a pawn in her parents' conflicts, Elena, although the principal character, functions primarily as an object of other people's interests. Her power to choose at the end of the story arises from her contact with natural scenes.[14]

Although the legal system is unnatural and destructive to human relationships, Elena's husband regards it highly. To him it is "what's left of divinity and not even a murderer would want to destroy divinity—not the last of it—even a murderer would draw back in reverence. We need what's holy. The law is holy. It will never be destroyed because there is no salvation outside it."[15] On the other hand, the system is, as far as he is concerned, dissociated from human life; the actual guilt and innocence of people are largely irrelevant to his profession.

Although Elena's lover, Jack, also thinks there is no salvation outside of the law, he becomes aware, especially during his work with racial discrimination in Mississippi, that there are kinds of injustices which the system cannot rectify. Further, Jack has premonitions of a violent overthrow of society. His yearning for an intimacy produced by turmoil is a distorted compensation for the alienation from life which, as a lawyer, he feels.

The reunion of Elena and Jack at the end of the novel seems an advance. A more positive relation to their circumstances is suggested by Jack's conclusion that life should not be a story which, like a legal case, is abstracted; rather, it should be a story "with surprising reversals and recognitions and coincidences."[16]

A major concern in these novels, that primary relationships become an obsession for people deprived of them, is central to *The Assassins*. The principal character, Andrew Petrie, has died, and in his absence his wife and brothers have nothing against which to prop up their lives. They fall into the vacancy he has left.

Andrew, a politician and a rationalist, believed that clarity of ideas dispensed with the need for God. Also a pessimist, he thought that the American experiment had failed—he was writing a book on the subject—and that global warfare was inevitable. Andrew was a powerful man physically, publicly, and intellectually.

When Andrew died, his brother Hugh lost his secure position in the world. A caricaturist, Hugh reduces people to their weaknesses and deformities. He feels protected from the threatening chaos of modern life by his art, and he seems to commit suicide in protest against the world. Although his profession is parasitic, Hugh feels godlike. His principal response to his brother's death is his attempt to become the lover of Andrew's widow. His inability to fill that position is confirmed when, having drugged Yvonne into submission, he finds himself impotent.

Yvonne continues to live in the apartment—her husband's room untouched—because she likes the isolation granted by its height. She is separated both from herself and from others. Although afflicted with vaginal bleeding, she is distant from her body and she observes herself in relation to other people as though watching a play. During a particularly vivid affair with her cousin, she is radically separated from herself, observing Harvey as he tries over and over again to achieve a climax.

Stephen, who has even less identity than do Hugh and Yvonne, feels connected with nothing. He considers himself to be an instance of God's presence, a medium or a vessel for an identity not his own. This does not necessarily mean that Stephen is more religious than the other characters; he seems no more involved in the funeral service or, later, in the Advent and Christmas seasons than the others. His mysticism is a peculiar form of alienation from the entire world, including himself.

Stephen is clearly a victim of unnatural family relations. Andrew had told him that he was conceived as the result of a contractual arrangement, money paid by his mother to his father for having another child because the other two children had disappointed her. Later his mother died, falling while drunk. Although she rejected him, Stephen misses her now that she is gone. And, of course, he has no relationship with his father.

These characters and others in the novel live in a serious state of deprivation from natural, particularly familial, relations. As a consequence, relationships based on compulsive dependence, coercion, hate, rejection, and ridicule arise.

The disconnections between people also affect the structure of Oates's novels. *Childwold*, for example, is a set of interior monologues without transitions or commentaries. This formal arrangement underscores the isolated positions of her characters.

In *Childwold* we also find children suffering deficiencies caused by parents who themselves experienced deprived childhoods. At forty-one, the wealthy Fitz-John Kasch is becoming more and more the son of a mother who denied the reality of the body; he increasingly withdraws from his historical and physical circumstances to match his earlier withdrawal into learning and books. And he uses his mind to become what he also lacked, his own father. Arlene Bartlett, forty, left her husband, Lyle, to live with her father. In turn, her father resents his own father deeply for having sent him, at the age of ten, to America to live with cousins. The place names—Eden County, Childwold, and Yewville—support the regressive tendencies of lives which suffer deficiencies in basic familial relationships.

In an attempt to compensate for these deficiencies, adults turn to extreme experiences. Unfed by his ordinary contacts with people, Kasch desires a violent sexual union with Arlene's teen-age daughter Evangeline, and he finds fulfillment in the struggle with, and brutal slaying of, Arlene's jealous former boyfriend, Earl Tuller. Arlene seems to come alive only in sexual acts and pregnancy; she has little if any interest in protracted relationships with men or with her many children.

Repulsed by her mother's child-crowded home, Evangeline is driven to Kasch because of her lack of a suitable father figure. She manipulates others, as do many of Oates's characters, by the same power which deprivation and withdrawal have had over her. Inadequate parents produce children who are never free from them and who perpetuate on their own children the faults which they have suffered.

Grotesque and extreme compensations or deprivations suffered in youth are also central to *Son of the Morning,* perhaps Oates's most subtle and complicated novel. Its point of view is complex, for the narrator renders an existence discontinuous with his present state; that is, he has become a person different from the self described.

The principal distinction between the narrator and his former self is that earlier he had been infused by the Holy Spirit but now stands bereft of that presence. And, as the author puts it, there is no one so lonely as a person who has once been fiercely loved by God and then abandoned by him. The impulse of the narrative act, therefore, is the experience of absence.

His burden, the narrator states, is to imagine this former self and the forceful reality of the presence of God. This he does in three ways. The isolation of the self from other people is, first of all, made clear. Raised by his grandmother, Nathanael Vickery is the illegitimate offspring of her gang-raped daughter, Eula. The grandmother uses Nathanael as an occasion to develop a spiritual life apart from and in defiance of her husband, a doctor by profession and a naturalist by conviction. This isolation from parental nurture and direction toward a religious life in Pentecostal and revivalistic contexts brings on seven instances of the presence of God.

Supporting the experience of God's presence is Nathanael's sense of American life. A sharp discontinuity is created between society and his experience, his ministry, and the religious sect he establishes. The devil has under his control American Society and all bodily functions and desires as well.

Finally, the experience of God's presence as a forceful reality is made clear by the use of prophetic and apocalyptic literature. The force and integrity of this material adds weight and historical depth to his expressions. While in other ways rather uneducated, Nathanael Vickery is an eloquent speaker, saturated with biblical material and convinced of his own role as a vessel of God's presence in the world.

The divine possession of Nathanael Vickery, although given content, is not advocated by the novel. This bizarre and extreme form of religious experience is rendered as the consequence of a secular world that has become devoid of presence and relationships. Nathanael's theology should be recognized as a function of the deprivation in his life. He insists, for example, on a docetic Christology, on the belief that Jesus only seemed to have a body. His understanding of the relation of spirit to body—as good to evil or as prisoner to cell—is gnostic. Although such a theology is not to be excluded from serious consideration, it is also clear that this form of religiousness is a function of Nathanael's separation from people. His sense of spiritual presence must be acknowledged as an alternative to the lack of presence in his social context, and that lack should be seen as continuous with his unnatural upbringing. The dedication of the novel —to the one who is, in absence, as palpable as any presence—suggests a presence which is known only after it is gone. Intense and bizarre forms of fulfillment, while understandable reactions to emptiness and deprivation, are desperate compensations for that which human life requires. Without primary human relationships, lives take on hideously unnatural shapes.

Unholy Loves reveals the absence of human interaction in a university community. The principal figure on campus for the year, the highly regarded English poet Albert St. Dennis has—in this his seventy-first year—no personal substance apart from the work he has done and the reputation which surrounds him. Although his presence provides members of the faculty an occasion for meeting and a common topic of conversation, he adds little to their lives. Even other artists, the novelist Brigit Stott and the composer Alexis Kessler, are not affected by contact with St. Dennis, although Kessler has written a set of songs for some of his poems. All of the academic people have unsatisfying relationships with their positions, with their families, and with one another. The ending of the work is more a rehearsal of what has been lost and of who has left than of what has been accomplished or gained.

In *Cybele*, mid-life crisis serves to reveal how attitudes bearing the potential for destruction can ultimately undo a person. Edwin Locke, at age forty-four, embarks on a two-year course of action which ends in his death. This period, while it seems to be a radical departure from his previous attitudes, is the result of his habit of hiding aspects of his life from outside view, of repressing his emotions, and of living in a state of alienation from others. In addition, he separates his present from his past. Mid-life crisis appears in this novel as the harvest of a life divided against itself. *Unholy Loves* and *Cybele*, thus, like other texts in Oates's corpus, are studies of adults distressed by a lack of community and integrity. This absence is caused by a loss of connections among aspects of a person's experience.

Bellefleur, Oates's most ambitious and only historical novel, depicts a family which immigrated to the United States in the 1770's. The correspondence in time between the arrival of the family and the beginnings of the nation suggests that the Bellefleurs and their history indirectly reveal something about American culture. Of the many characteristics of the family, three are most noteworthy.

First, they and the narrative resist the flow of time. Characters and events are not presented in chronological order; rather, chapters dealing with various moments in the Bellefleur history are juxtaposed. Also, cause and effect are less sequential than dialectical. For example, characters either affirm Bellefleur interests or recoil from them. Furthermore, the family is closely identified with the house which was built by its most ambitious member, Raphael, in the mid-nineteenth century. The house is peopled with the ghostly presences of its former inhabitants and furnished with such reminders of them as the drum made from Raphael's skin. The living and the dead are simultaneous. The principal way in which time is retarded and a synchronic or spatial view given is through the repetition of a major event, the destruction of the family and the survival of one of its members, a female named Germaine.

A second characteristic of the household and, by implication of American culture, is its lack of historical grounding. The Bellefleurs, who left France in the eighteenth century, took little of their culture with them. Consequently, there is little content to their history except style and strategy, both being rapacious. The family has no cultural grounding of its own and is closed to influences from without. The Bellefleurs have exploited the land and its inhabitants.

Third, the family tends toward spiritualism and disembodiment as compensation for its materialism and brutality. While this spiritualist leaning often has a Christian or biblical articulation, it is privately mystical and generated by a revulsion against temporality and carnality. Jedediah, to whom many of the chapters are devoted, pursues an ascetically mystical existence in the mountains during the early part of the nineteenth century. His son Raphael, while ambitious for worldly gain, is also repulsed by physicality and prefers the purity of dollars. The pattern continues in the twentieth century: Vernon, the poet, thinks of himself as a fragment of God's consciousness; and Leah's husband, Gideon, becomes a pilot in order to reject the earth. Compensating for this spiritual direction are moves by some family members to the darkness or the fecundity of the earth, such as young Raphael's fascination for the pond and Yolande's interest in the cemetery.

The Bellefleur family, like every family, has its own destructive tendencies. Leah's estrangement from Gideon, lack of an adequate father, attachment to cats and spiders, and obsession with her youngest child, as well as Gideon's insatiable need for other women and suicidal plane crash into the Bellefleur castle, are all patterns of behavior which arise from inadequate or distorted primary relationships. But the family has wider connections: the Indians whom they exploited, the Blacks whom they tortured, and the poor whom they disdained. These external relationships indicate the burden of guilt and enmity which continues to deform the Bellefleurs and, we can conclude, Americans in general.

The characters in the fiction of Joyce Carol Oates live in a world that has become unnatural due to the loss of primary human relations. This loss accompanies the abstraction of individual consciousness from the nexus of interaction and the removal of relatedness from human life. The effect of these novels is not primarily to arouse our sympathy for characters so situated; rather, the reader is led to conclude that moral and spiritual health is rooted, at a minimum, in relationships free from these subjugations, perversions, and withdrawals. Viewing the consequences of the loss of primary relationships, the reader, by a process of imaginative inversion, can recognize the values of wholesome, creative interdependence not only between individuals but also between people and their natural and historical environments. The individual becomes human if deprivations in his past do not force him to turn on others as a means of satisfaction or advancement. The use of character by Oates is a negative exposure of the belief that the natural world we have lost and must regain is the world of human, particularly familial, relationships.

4

John Gardner's Pastoral Apocalypticism

The characters in John Gardner's fiction face the end of their careers, are near death, or live on the fringes of society. Unlike those more securely positioned, these characters stand unprotected from threatening but finally inescapable truths. The exposure granted by their vulnerability does not frighten Gardner's characters but engages them more freely in life. They undergo experiences which lead to what William James sees as the fruit of conversion, a feeling of being at home in the universe.

Most of Gardner's characters, because they are old or ill, are in the process of accepting their own dying. This process has profound consequences for their sense of position in the world. For example, they tend to become less self-centered or self-protective, more flexible, more observant of the needs and follies of people around them, and more charitable than they were before. Their responses to the human capacity to foresee death distinguish them from characters who conclude that their own dying signals the end of the world, resist all change, or become violent. But the main characters find—through the discipline of facing the end—wisdom, moral and spiritual freedom, and health which they had not previously known.

James Chandler, the protagonist of *The Resurrection*, illustrates this conversion to life at the point of death. A professor of philosophy and an academically righteous Job, Chandler, at the age of forty-one, learns that his world, ordered by a philosophical method, an agenda of problems, and a style of writing which gives him a sense of "perfect control,"[1] has been undercut by leukemia. "The limits of Chandler's identity (It was thus that he put it to himself, fleeing into the comforting arms of pedantic abstractions) were set."[2] Remarkably, Chandler allows the knowledge of his dying to affect his life, to dissolve his sense of control, to change his relationships with others, and even to alter his epistemology. Rather than resent and repress the knowledge or turn in nihilistic judgment on the entire world, he allows it to grant him a new life in relation to others and to his environment; his conversion is, as the title of the book suggests, a resurrection to life.

By moving with his family to Batavia, New York, Chandler encounters responses to death not concealed by the intellectual sophistication and abstraction of academia. One reaction is provided by three elderly aunts who have retreated from life and who preserve their dwindling existence in a mausoleum of stasis. In their overheated, antiquely furnished home, they retain the illusion of artistic permanence. These precious ladies, like untouched old lace, crumble under too much exposure or when the preservative of their schedules is lost.

Other responses are suggested in the attitudes of Chandler's mother, Rose, and of his wife, Marie. These women are more distant from Chandler than their positions would suggest. Rose identifies death with natural processes like weather because she underestimates the distinctly human capacity to foresee and to reflect on one's own dying. Marie's attitude toward dying has been determined by a childhood experience: she caused the death of a lost boy by selfishly failing to admit that she had seen him. Her protection from the reality of death takes the form of superficiality and efficiency; she is a person who "judged the right and wrong of a point on some such grounds as whether or not *The New Yorker* would be likely to mock it."[3]

A more complicated response to the knowledge of one's own dying is provided by John Horne, an embodiment of the Sartrean dissociation of the transcendent ego from an almost nauseatingly huge, odoriferous, and dying body. For Horne, one's own dying is not a kind of knowledge but is, rather, a fact about life to which knowledge forms a counterpart and a defense. His life, he admits, is "All strictly theoretical."[4] Despite his comments on mystery and sacrifice, Horne's response to dying is the flight of consciousness from the circumstances of life.

The responses of Viola, the spinsters' niece, to Chandler's dying are even more complicated. At first she reacts out of a generally morbid fascination for death. As a young girl, she had seen her father in his casket and envied him. So, like sensation seekers who are drawn to accidents, Viola is stimulated by Chandler's fall in the street. This morbidity is exacerbated by her tendency—made clear by the scene with Marie in the park and by her intention to kill Chandler—to turn life into drama. But in her, too, a genuine affection for the Chandler family develops: ". . . it had been at the Chandlers', where it was important to be listening every minute for a child's cry—listening even while she slept—and where responsibilities kept her running from dawn to dark, that she had felt, for the first time in her life, really free, really happy."[5] This ability to be changed by circumstances grants Viola stature and allows her to provide the occasion for Chandler's dying act.

Chandler learns that life is both complicated and enriched by human experiences. Developing neither an intellectual response to his dying nor an aesthetic feeling about the mystery and beauty of life, he ends simply with an acceptance, even a celebration, of *"the world*, the buzzing blooming confusion itself."[6] His resurrection is to a human life that is more complex and primary than we normally assume. Dying, when it undermines avoidances of life, can be a form of knowledge revealing that we do not die like animals, as Rose believes, or like abstracted consciousnesses merely observing the fact, as Horne would have it. The image of human possibilities rendered through Chandler is of the person neither reduced by dying nor alienated from his life, neither self-preserving nor destructive toward himself or others. Rather, he is awakened by dying to a truer knowledge of his own life, a more charitable relationship with others, and an acceptance of his world.

Matters are a bit more strained in *The Wreckage of Agathon* because the principal character here, while also facing his own death, feels a sharper conflict between himself and the society around him. Although his awareness of dying makes Agathon sensitive to temporal flux and to the complexity and uncertainty of human life, the world epitomized by Lykourgos is oriented to stasis, perpetuity, and decorum. This conflict lends severity to Agathon's position on the fringe of society.

In addition to the contrast provided by Lykourgos, the character of Agathon is also clarified by a contrary juxtaposition with the religiously saintly Dorkis. Agathon says of him,

> I was impressed; in fact, awed. Shackled, beaten, Dorkis seemed more powerful than all of them. It seemed to me for an instant that he had learned something of unspeakable importance, but the next instant I doubted that—it was my silly philosopher's prejudice that power comes from knowledge. It struck me (God knows what I meant by it) that Something had learned Dorkis. It was as if one of his gods had gotten inside him, had taken over.[7]

This comment makes Dorkis the contrary of Lykourgos who fashions his world, the city, into an image of himself. Between these two characters, Agathon stands as one who, knowing he cannot shape death into his own image, allows the process to affect his life. He is a seer and a recorder of forces on him; "Time is a matter of the greatest perplexity,"[8] he says, and it must be lived in as a primary and uncertain reality. In Gardner's fictional world, some individuals are capable of doing that.

Gardner's interest in life on the fringes of society appears again in his depiction of Grendel, the monster of the epic poem *Beowulf*. From the perspective of the monster, Hrothgar's court and the orientation to life it represents are not so attractive. These "thinking creatures, pattern makers,"[9] hack down trees and blister the land "till the forest looked like an old dog dying of mange."[10] Worst of all—and this is one of many antiaesthetic points in Gardner's fiction —this violence is transformed by poets into lovely verses and celebrated in song.

Such human behavior arises in part because man is defensive— afraid of and violent toward the natural powers in his world which he can neither predict nor control. Despite Grendel's defeat, his opposition to mankind will continue.[11] Grendel and human culture conflict because of their contrary attitudes toward life and its meaning. Humans destroy in order to replace the world as it is with a world they can understand and control; for Grendel the natural world is a "mechanical chaos of casual, brute enmity on which we stupidly impose our hopes and fears."[12] This state of opposition finds an alternative in Beowulf, here more indefinite and more discontinuous with the world around him than the hero of the original epic. He says to Grendel, "It's coming, my brother. Believe it or not. Though you murder the world, turn plains to stone, transmogrify life into I and it, strong searching roots will crack your cave and rain will cleanse it: the world will burn green, sperm build again. My promise."[13] Antagonist to both Grendel and the Danes, Beowulf stands as spokesman for human life revitalized by a relation with natural forces.

Characters who represent contrary and equally mistaken positions on the question of man's relation to nature appear as well in *The Sunlight Dialogues*. Here we find two men who are inevitable contraries: Fred Clumly, the police chief of Batavia, New York, and Taggert Hodge, proponent of love and inhabitant of the fringes of Batavian society. Clumly, nearing retirement, has exhausted himself by trying to protect Batavia from the chaos that he thinks increasingly marks American life. For him, Taggert epitomizes all that threatens traditional values: "Scrape together the Sunlight Man's secrets, and you'd have in your hands a collection of horrors, it might be, that would knock a common mortal on his hiney."[14] Taggert proves not to represent the kind of anarchy and hedonism Clumly associates with California but, rather, to have a genuine interest in other people. Clumly learns this through their dialogues. Taggert contends that, while the police chief is oriented to the sky, he is oriented to the earth; while Clumly is interested in law and control, Taggert is open to spontaneity, individuality, and earthly energy.

Taggert's family, once large and respected, has declined, and its demise coincides with that of civilization.

> But subtly, so subtly that no one had noticed the thing as it happened, the might of the Hodges had sifted between their fingers. Betrayed by life itself. The richest farm country in New York State had mysteriously grayed: the land had quit; stone fences had fallen into disrepair; the Guernsey dairies—best dairies in the world—had begun to give way to Holstein dairies, quantity over quality; and then price supports came. . . .[15]

That the present is a sad, gray time is also evident in the depictions of minor characters: Boyle is a thief because he has no respect for the world in which he lives; the Paxton women are victims of an unhealthy family and society; the Woodworths' life has slipped beneath them; a psychiatrist admits his admiration for experiments done in German concentration camps; Freeman, himself an unsocialized person, acts out of a social concern that is masked sentimentality; and a Chicago friend of Will Hodge, Jr., unwittingly caricatures himself by extolling the pleasures of sex with six women at one time. Even the narrator steps aside from the consciousnesses of his characters to provide a wider perspective on the situation:

> Unbeknownst to Clumly or anyone else, three boys in the alley by the post office were letting the air out of people's tires with an ice pick. Elsewhere—beside the Tonawanda—a woman was digging a grave for her illegitimate child three hours old. Jim Hume was chasing the cows back through the fence some hunter had cut. There was no moon.[16]

The evil of the social context, therefore, is not simply a projection by Clumly. While Taggert responds to this situation by trying to turn society toward a spontaneous naturalism, Clumly reacts by attempting to conserve values and an order from which society has lapsed. But because of Taggert's influence, Clumly turns toward more charitable ends. Less and less anxious about his retirement, he becomes able to affirm the value of individuality. Yet Taggert is not a completely reliable guide concerning man's relation to nature; the world is not, as he thinks, a street where all the lights are green. Clumly comes to recognize that although the human tasks of judging and discriminating cannot, as Taggert believes, be abandoned, the natural depths of life and of human relationships can be trusted. Clumly is softened and complicated by his recognition of the inherent mystery from which life arises and to which it must regularly return. This is nicely suggested by his new relation to his wife. During their long marriage they had grown increasingly separated, a situation aggravated by her blindness. But toward the end of the narrative Clumly gains a new appreciation for her, one described by reference to his treasured but brief career as a sailor. "He had an image of a calm and placid sea where nothing stirred, where the water was clear and pointlessly beautiful, but always darker than a man imagined, and down inside its darkness things were stirring, omens and portents. To tell the truth, he did not know her."[17] The tie to this earlier experience unifies Clumly's life.

The characters depicted in *Nickel Mountain* also possess a sense of the present as treacherous. Although subtitled *A Pastoral Novel*, this work is heavy with catastrophe. Old Kuzitski dies when his truck goes off the road; the Bale's house burns, and the wife dies in the fire; Bale himself suffers a fatal fall on Henry Soames's stairway; George Loomis lost a foot in the Korean war and a hand in a farm machine; the Goat Lady is killed when struck from behind by George's car; Willard Freund, hitchhiking, barely escapes death, while the driver of the car does not; and at the end, an elderly couple disinter the remains of their fourteen-year-old son, who years ago had been killed by lightning. There are other disconcerting details: Callie's long and painful labor, the dead rabbit, the story of the Sprague brothers who fall victim to fratricide, and the violent temper of Henry Soames.

Some of the characters draw apocalyptic or otherwise nihilistic conclusions about life when it is marked by natural catastrophe and moral evil. First among these characters is Simon Bale, a Jehovah's Witness, who, as a night clerk in a cheap urban hotel, received a close view of human evil and who witnesses door-to-door about the proximity of the end time. George Loomis, at least at one point, tends to agree with Bale: "People are no damn good."[18] Loomis has retreated from life and lives alone on a mountain surrounded by his collection of things. Even young Freund believed that "the stupidity of American democracy, was going to destroy the world—and soon."[19]

This is the context Gardner provides his principal character, Henry Soames, the proprietor of an all-night diner on the highway. Henry feels close to death because of his obesity and weak heart, but the apocalyptic attitudes of people around him find a contrast in supportive natural settings. The condition of never being closed (which characterizes Henry's work) and his orientation to nature allow him to receive young Callie into his life one spring after a long and increasingly darkening period of discouragement. Callie's arrival and Henry's ability to accept her produce new life and growth in him. This does not mean that Henry is unaware of threats in his environment: the dark and forbidding woods, the winter cold, and the loneliness and dinginess of the diner; but by trusting circumstances, he dissolves his fears.

The ambiguities of Henry's world match his own complex nature: his charity and his temper, his interests in other people and his suicidal tendencies, his openness to the world outside his diner and his anxiety about what lies out there. By responding to Callie, Henry permits himself to become a friend, allows the husband to be drawn out of him, and becomes a father and son-in-law. Despite his rather stationary and heavy presence, new possibilities are created in him by circumstances. This creative relation to life's processes becomes quite clear in Henry's encounter with young Freund, who recognizes that Henry has become the father because of his care for Callie and the child. Henry comments that when a person recognizes that he cannot be adequate to those he loves, he begins to realize who God is. In the face of inadequacy some become defensive. But the capacity for personal growth is granted to those who give themselves to the changes which life's uncertainties require.

In *October Light*, Gardner, as he does in other works, presents two characters with contrary but equally mistaken attitudes toward the natural circumstances of human life. They end their conflict by dissolving their resistance to one another and to life around them, and this resolution is stimulated primarily by exposure to dying.

It is October, and Vermont Yankee James Page, born on the fourth of July seventy-two years ago, puts on a face appropriate for the approaching Halloween, a face that will frighten off the evil spirits which he thinks pervade the land. As the story progresses, however, he learns that the ghosts are not only outside of his life, in the cheap and dishonest culture that television most clearly represents; they are within him and his past as well. The conversion he must undergo involves relinquishing his resentment of the changes produced by time.

When he destroys his older sister's television set and chases her to her room with a stick, James's longstanding frustrations erupt. Besieged by a culture toward which he has felt increasingly hostile, he reacts violently to his sister's act of bringing the enemy into his home. Aggravating this sense of crisis is James's conclusion that time is running out on him and on the values he represents. His daughter Virginia, while very much on the scene, grants little hope for the future because James has a low opinion of women and shares few interests with her husband. James is a desperate man engaged in an ideological last stand in which his personal investment is enormous.

His sister Sally, locked in her room, is isolated from the world because of a very different agenda. She does not regret the loss of the past on account of its righteousness; rather, she recalls her former life with her sophisticated and disillusioned husband as a world of lost opportunities. She had been a warmblooded young woman, and she resents the restraint that the good old days forced on her sensual life. Consequently, her voluntary captivity is directed less against James than toward a fantasy world of separate and intense gratification, a world amply supported by the trashy novels she reads. This novel—another of Gardner's antiaesthetic moments—deals with a withdrawn and indulgent community of marijuana smugglers. It concludes with the flight of two characters from the drugged and sex-filled underworld to some other Eden in space. Sally, as troubled by diarrhea as James is by constipation, is the contrary of her brother and is equally mistaken.

For James Page, life is "a brief and hopeless struggle against the pull of the earth."[20] Attitudes and ideas current in the culture conceal this truth by granting an "illusion of freedom and ascent."[21] Sally wants such an ascent; she creates through reading an imaginary world in which she feels "godlike." In order for these characters to end the stalemate, both must attain a new relation to the circumstances they share. Sally must recognize that her ascent is hurtful to others, and James must recognize that his involvement in the lives around him makes his isolation and sense of superiority illusory.

While specific events occasion the changes both undergo, the needed transformations are produced primarily by relatives, neighbors, and friends. Despite their self-preoccupation, self-pity, and mutual hostility, James and Sally are upheld by a strong current of concern, respect, and even affection from people who form the human environment of their lives.

Commentary accompanies their transformations. The sermon given by the pastor in the hallway reaches the conclusion: "Times change, then; that is the lesson of our text, God's first great book, as Aquinas called it, 'The Book of Nature.' "[22] James then realizes "the bitterness was that he felt like a young man, trapped inside this wrecked and dying body. . . . He was like the young parrot at the Arlington House, screaming with holy indignation in his cage while the hotel burned down around him."[23] Indirect commentary on the attitudes of the main characters is provided by descriptions of Ed Thomas's dying.

When James recognizes the violence of which he is capable and the losses which he has perpetrated on himself, he also recognizes that not all of the ghosts are evil spirits. After he has "fallen back into the world, found the magic door,"[24] he sees his dead wife's face again. The vision reminds him that "life had been good once, that life *was* good, as poor Ed Thomas understood now more clearly than ever, now that he was dying."[25]

Gardner's interest in character, then, reveals that life can be rejuvenated and refreshed if individuals attain what William James calls a feeling of being at home in the universe. Awareness of death is, for Gardner, the primary occasion for conversion to this positive attitude. As stated in *Nickel Mountain*, "A bad heart was the beginning of wisdom."[26] The ability to allow time and circumstances to change and re-create oneself is wisdom.

Like the works of Mailer and Oates, Gardner's fiction—while by no means in the same way or with the same emphasis—renders characters whose lives are threatened by a divorce from natural realities and resources, characters who must come once again into a primary relationship with a context which is not the product of human design or control. Because of this way of construing moral and spiritual dilemmas and possibilities, Gardner's fiction should be grouped with that of other writers we have mentioned in this part, Herman Melville, Mark Twain, Ernest Hemingway, William Styron, Susan Sontag, and others. Furthermore, all these writers share the general diagnosis of the human condition articulated in the works of William James, Henry Nelson Wieman, and Bernard Meland. Finally, these writers and thinkers stand before us as representatives of one of three ways in which Americans tend to come to grips with the moral and spiritual nature of human life.

PART TWO

THE MARGINAL MAN

5

Conflict and Interpretation

The second belief shaping character in American fiction construes the major threat to human life not as confinement within a humanly controlled world but as cultural conflict. The solution to the problem lies not in a contact with natural realities, but in the overcoming of conflict through interpretation. Crucial to the solution is the belief that both or all parties in the conflict have values which should be preserved in the resolution and that the future is able to accommodate them. Before discussing the role of this belief in the works of three contemporary authors, we shall examine it as a dimension of American culture, as it appears in major texts in the narrative tradition, and as it affects the work of representative American theologians.

It may seem strange to identify one kind of character in American literature with a cultural concern. Indeed, critics of American fiction tend to assume that its intensely individuated, alienated characters engage in a rejection of society. Surely this is often true, particularly with characters who, as we saw in the preceding chapter, attempt to make contact with nature. But some characters, far from rejecting culture, may suffer alienation because of their attempt to affirm two or more often conflicting cultures. While alienation may be identifiable in characters of the first and third types, those affected by the belief which we are now trying to expose are distressed because they are too involved in culture; they are trying to reconcile or to re-create its conflicting elements in their own experience. It is to such an individual that the title of this section, "The Marginal Man," refers.

Everett Stonequist illuminates the causes and consequences of personally felt cultural conflict. He defines the marginal man as an individual who, because of migration, education, marriage, or some other influence, leaves one social group or culture and enters another. Such an individual is too indebted to the culture he leaves and too deeply impressed by the one he enters to solve the problem of their noncompatibility by rejecting one for the sake of the other. Thus he is only partially extricated from one culture and only partially assimilated into another. While wholly at ease in neither, he derives his identity from both.

The marginal man, according to Stonequist, will often be creative. In order to make sense of his world, he must constantly attempt to resolve the ambiguities created by the affirmation of two conflicting cultures. His distance from both the culture which he attempts to adopt and the one which he leaves behind is taxing. Yet, it is also stimulating. If the marginal man has energy for the task, he will affirm his unique hybrid identity and explain himself to others as well as to himself. In his experience, reflection, and interpretation he will hammer out a new phenomenon: the unique blend of two conflicting cultures.

In addition to being creative, the marginal man is also critical. Because the values of one culture will sensitize him to the deficiencies and even evils of the other, he will be aware—as those around him may not be—of the limitations and objectionable aspects of both his adopted and his forfeited homes. When a person moves from one culture to another without wholly rejecting either, he is, says Stonequist, both potentially creative and astutely critical. "The marginal man is the key-personality in the contacts of cultures. It is in his mind that the cultures come together, conflict, and eventually work out some kind of mutual adjustment and interpretation. He is the crucible of cultural fusion."[1] Although individuated by virtue of his dual identity, the marginal man is yet committed, perhaps overcommitted, to culture.

The threat to personal integrity which these conditions raise can be, of course, very great. The validation of personal life is possible only if a resolution to the conflict is found. The threat must be met with more than ongoing adjustments; response depends on faith in a future to which the process of interpretation leads.

Cultural conflict and the need for interpretation is a paradigm with deep roots in American experience. It arises from the mobility of individuals and groups in our society.

Conflict is also a part of American experience because the society is constituted of people from many cultures. Although such conflict was particularly intensified by immigration during the final quarter of the nineteenth century and the early decades of the twentieth, it is limited neither to this moment in our history nor to the so-called second generation.[2] The sense of cultural conflict is deeply ingrained because of the weight and prestige of the European culture which most Americans both left behind and brought with them.[3] While the intensity of this conflict between the components which form any American's social identity may vary from rather slight to excruciating, to be American is, at the same time, to be something else.

Furthermore, Americans experienced the consequences of that great cultural ground-shift which created, in the seventeenth century, an anthropocentric world which opposed an ecclesiastically or divinely ordered one. The settling of our land occurred simultaneously with this great change, and American social and political structures are inconceivable apart from it. But this separation or conflict was, as Marius Bewley notes,[4] largely unmediated by institutions; Americans felt it more personally and with greater force than did their European counterparts. Thus, the split created was less between separate institutions than between components of a person's own life, especially between private and public selves. To be an American, even one not affiliated with a religious organization, is to feel some sense of conflict between personal values and the public, value-free domain.[5]

Cultural conflict also arises from contrary understandings of the directions and goals of American life. Do they lie in a fresh beginning? in simplicity? in an Edenic society free from governmental control and cultural coercion? Or, do they exist in a future that the impact of a new technology on the naturally rich soil produces? As Leo Marx says, the machine and the garden represent the conflict of "Technology and the Pastoral Ideal in America."[6] This tension we continue to feel, perhaps more acutely now than ever before.

To be both American and indebted to some other culture, to be divided between a private and a public world, to drive a machine and to cultivate the simple life—these are among the major antinomies of American life. They carry profound moral and spiritual consequences, and a resolution to them is vital to the integrity or wholeness of personal identity.

Character in American fiction has been, and continues to be, formed by the beliefs that cultural conflict is a threat to personal integrity, that it requires interpretation, and that the future is able to accommodate the values of cultures in tension. The presence of these beliefs makes American fiction less anarchical or narcissistic than it is generally thought to be; our national literature has been deeply involved in the work of cultural fusion. Marginal men, to use Stonequist's words, are crucibles of cultural fusion and harbingers of a larger cultural future. Among major narratives in which character is developed according to this belief are *The Scarlet Letter,* *The Wings of the Dove,* and *Absalom, Absalom!*

Seventeenth-century Boston fascinates the narrator of *The Scarlet Letter* because it is a setting in which cultural conflicts as well as their resolutions can be felt. This moment in American history seems marked, also, by contact between two worlds—Medieval and Reformation Christianity (Dimmesdale is related to both) and the emerging rationalism and empiricism (represented by Chillingworth). These two ideologies, together with the romantic leanings of Hester, continued in the narrator's own day. Nathaniel Hawthorne uses character to epitomize conflicting cultures which have a potentially destructive relationship. Within this situation of cultural conflict tensions also appear between law and charity, self and society, male and female, art and religion, and the fanciful and the real.

The narrator of *The Scarlet Letter* is sensitive to cultural conflict because he is himself a marginal man. Returning to the place of his origins after a period of absence, he views his situation with a critical scrutiny others lack. He feels, as he had not previously, the tug of his ancestral roots. His sympathy for his material is largely a readiness to affirm the value of conflicting parties. The attitude is both aesthetic and moral. Sympathy is not simply a will toward unity; it arises from a belief that beyond life's conflicts are "Remarkable Providences"—to use the title words of Increase Mather's book of 1683. Human life is affirmed as providentially unified in ways that poetic insight may be able to intuit.[7]

Another form of cultural conflict found in this narrative is the relation of the present to the past.[8] For Hawthorne this was an urgent problem, for it involved his attachment to and alienation from both the seventeenth and the nineteenth centuries.[9] Despite the obstacles, a sense of wholeness with the past must be forged, because to lack paternity and a past is to live incompletely. While they may constitute a problem for us, fathers provide the cultural conditions in which we are nurtured and out of which we must emerge; the past gives weight and mystery to personal life.

It may appear that the narrative does no more than uncover the tragic conflicts by which existence is torn and distressed. It could be argued that the "religious obligation" of the writer is to use character in order to introduce the reader to life's "dark necessity" and to depict experience as "multiplicity inherent in apparent unity."[10] For such a reading, Hawthorne, "rather than attempting to reduce complexity to unity and by so doing to arrive at a knowledge of the guiding principle behind apparent opposites . . . accepts these opposites, these apparent contradictions, and studies them in and for themselves."[11] While there seems to be little doubt that Hawthorne's characters are occasions of cultural conflict, there is room for disagreement as to whether or not conflict is the last word in this narrative. Rather than see them as fragmented, we may view his characters as shaped by the belief that human life, so in conflict with itself, is also, by remarkable providence, called toward unity. It is on such a belief that the characters, the sympathy of narrator and reader, and the wholeness of the romance is based.

Characters in Henry James's *The Wings of the Dove* are manifestations of differing cultures; their conflicts result less from personal than from cultural misalignments. The Americans view Europe as a cultural ideal and refuge, a place where—primarily through the reading of fiction—they aspire to find acceptance. Armed with these expectations, they tend to be innocent of the complexities and ambiguities of English life. Schooled by opportunity and empowered by wealth, Americans possess an exuberance which stands in potential conflict with the attitudes or manners of Europeans, whose lives are shaped by a denser and more refined society. Their English hosts and friends appear more practical. They have to negotiate obstacles which, while often serious, must not trouble the calm surface of an elegant social style. The commercial and diplomatic imagery James uses to describe their personal relations underscores the matter. Practical and social exigencies tend to render these English hosts unprepared for the gratuitous or extravagant acts of their American guests.

The conflicts caused by cultural differences are exacerbated by additional contrarieties: necessity and luxury, desire and sacrifice, expediency and virtue, good for self and good for others, deception and truth, death and life, abyss and height. Of these pairs the most important one seems to be the conflict between power and love.

From the perspective of Merton Densher—and it seems unavoidable in commenting on the work of James that the perspective of one of the characters must be assumed—there are three kinds of power in the world. Densher is related in a mutually complicating way to all three. The first, social and economic power, presided over by that epitome of London society Maud Lowder, is Lancaster Gate, and the name suggests that of the three kinds of power this one allows for easiest entry. But social and economic power, though in appearance large and accommodating, is the least charitable. Merton enters an unaccepting world there, and Maud expects that he will end his involvement with Kate either because of his own ingenuous lack of ambition or because of an awareness that he is not what is best for her. Maud assumes that the power conferred by social position transcends human relations. The widest passage becomes the narrowest when social power is used to determine personal life.

The second form of power which Merton experiences is sexual. Kate uses this power to move matters according to her supposedly charitable intentions to do what is best for everybody. Actually, she trades on Merton's sexual desire as a way of manipulating the situation. The matter becomes most explicit when she gives herself to Merton in exchange for his acquiescence to her scheme.

The third kind of power, aesthetic and spiritual, is typified by Milly. Entry to this force is as narrow and virginal as the unopened envelope of her final, creative gesture. Her act transcends the conflict between power and love. Under the guidance, it seems, of Sir Luke Strett and in response to the bitter facts of her own approaching death and betrayal, Milly alters the situation by the power of a transforming love. She is most beautiful in her last, dying act, and its power is felt by others: "We shall never be again as we were!"[12] As an answer to conflict, spiritual power does not change characters into something less than themselves.

Few characters typify the role of the marginal man in American fiction better than William Faulkner's Quentin Compson in *Absalom, Absalom!* A Mississippi boy in a cold dormitory room at Harvard, he tries to make sense of his almost incomprehensible origins with the help of his marginal friend, the Canadian, Shreve. The movement of the book is produced by their interpretations of the Sutpen-Coldfield history. Their labor is a creative act because it results in a viable whole.

Creativity is necessary not only because some of the facts are missing but also because the narrative comes from conflicting sources. For Quentin's father the story is problematic; he cannot unify all of its elements and, what is more important, he tends to support Sutpen's actions and attitudes. Furthermore, Mr. Compson has the benefit of Sutpen's own explanation of his motives. Rosa's view conflicts with Compson's. She is unable to complete the imaginative act not because she lacks imagination, like Mr. Compson, but because she is too involved, too vindictive toward Sutpen. In addition, Rosa is a product of a "closed masonry of females," and there are few symptoms of a distressed culture more important in Faulkner's fiction than the destructive conflict and isolation between men and women. Rosa's attitude toward men, particularly toward her father and Sutpen, is one of disdain and even revulsion.

Principally at stake, then, is the act of the creative imagination, making a whole cloth out of the pieces granted by conflicting parties. This dimension of the novel is supported by details in the story itself. The three young people are products of an unfruitful conflict between the male and female worlds. Quentin, himself reared in such a domestic situation, well can sympathize with the distortions produced in these children, particularly in Henry. The characters and their relationships are not presented as psychological case studies; rather, they are products of a culture divided against itself. As the biblical allusion in the title suggests, houses divided cannot continue to stand.

Sutpen, a product of cultural conflict, combines aristocratic ambitions with frontier manners. A hard-working, uncomplaining, and convivial man, he is trying to raise himself to a higher social level. Yet, in his use of those who work for him, in his attitudes toward the land, and in his relationships with individual women he is violent and self-serving. Sutpen's complex personality also produces contrary reactions in others. He stimulates a raging resentment in Rosa, whereas the male population of the county finds him attractive, as his friendship with old Compson, the cooperation of Mr. Coldfield, and the successful stag parties at his house indicate.

The conflict between cultures is seen not only in the juxtaposition of the Sutpen story to the Harvard setting and in the antagonisms between men and women, it is also found in the relationship of the present to the past. Sutpen's unfortunate rejection of aspects of his past typifies the failure of the white South to take seriously the presence of black people. This unrecognized problem in Southern history leads to Shreve's judgment that the Jim Bonds will conquer the Western Hemisphere. Quentin, while he tries valiantly to interpret his past, has been too weakened by it to complete the work of forging an identity in the crucible of cultural conflicts.

The interpretation of marginality shapes character in these novels as well as in the fiction of more recent authors. J. F. Powers, who grew up as a Catholic in a southern Illinois Protestant town, creates characters, usually priests, who try to make some kind of connection with the surrounding, largely non-Catholic world. Peter De Vries was too influenced by his Dutch Reformed upbringing on the near-west side of Chicago to accept uncritically the plastic superficiality of Connecticut suburbia; his characters and narrators are astute observers of the empty provincialism of an affluent but spiritless America. John Updike sets most of his fiction in the gap between the values of a pastoral, Protestant past and the problems of a spiritually disoriented, East-coast sophistication. Jewish writers deal primarily with characters who are marginal people; examples are S. Levin off in Cascadia in Bernard Malamud's *A New Life* and Yasha Mazur in Warsaw in Isaac Singer's *The Magician of Lublin*. Furthermore, although racism is more important than cultural conflict for the formation of characters in fiction by Black Americans, the marginal man is also detectable in such works as *Native Son* and *Invisible Man*.

Cultural conflict, with the need for its interpretation, is a problem pervasive in our culture. The relation of cultural conflict to belief is clarified by the religious anthropologies of representative thinkers, such as Walter Rauschenbusch, Reinhold Niebuhr, and Langdon Gilkey.

Rauschenbusch recognizes the potential of religion for creating cultural cohesion. In his work, which culminates in *Theology for the Social Gospel*, there is an enthusiasm for actualizing in contemporary America a potential in Christianity which the church has neglected since the life of Jesus.[13] Indeed, according to Rauschenbusch, the great error of Christian history has been its tendency to accept and to aggravate divisions among people. Theology in modern America, however, has the unique role of reviving the message that God is immanent in humanity and is providing the means for reconciliation between people now separated. Rauschenbusch views the central emphasis of Christianity to be "humanity as a great solidarity and God indwelling in it."[14] The antagonism among individuals and among groups is an evil he finds rooted in the selfish aggravation of differences. Redemption is a process which allows society to resemble a family, and Rauschenbusch expects this fruit of Christianity from the soil of American democracy.

According to Reinhold Niebuhr, the problem is a deeper and more desperate situation than Rauschenbusch acknowledges. For Niebuhr, cultural conflicts attach themselves to ontological contraries in human life. Much of *The Nature and Destiny of Man* depicts the inability of philosophical and theological anthropologies either to face these contraries or to solve the problems they create. This universal faultfinding would be subject to Gustave Weigel's charge of arrogance[15] were Niebuhr prepared to provide an alternative solution. But for Niebuhr, there are no final answers.

Niebuhr's interest in cultural conflict can also be seen in his discussion of the dismantled Thomistic synthesis. A conflict arose between two aspects of Western culture: the Renaissance emphasis on human initiative and the Reformation's stress on man's need for divine grace. This separation aggravates the ontological contraries, and it greatly exacerbates the theological burden.

Although for Niebuhr the problems arising from human nature in conflict with itself are extreme, the situation is not hopeless. He contends that man has a capacity for self-correction. A partial understanding of human nature leads to the recognition of those sides of life which have been excluded or ignored. In addition, man can see his own and his community's limitations and mistakes. He has the ability to transcend himself, to imagine a new society, and to revise his goals.

The answer to the anxiety which arises out of the conflicts within human life is faith in God, "the ground and source of the temporal."[16] God gives meaning to incoherent events by comprehending them simultaneously, even as human consciousness activates unity and meaning in segments through memory and foresight.[15] While sin contradicts the true nature of time and causes God's work to suffer,[17] acts of love, like their christological paradigm, generate power and validity by granting access to the reconciling, divine mercy.

Cultural conflict and interpretation are also central matters for Langdon Gilkey. The intention of his most important book *Naming the Whirlwind: The Renewal of God-Language* is to develop a religious anthropology from two divided aspects of human life: experience and religious inheritance. He sees the problem of religious anthropology to be our inability to speak about human experiences of finality and depth. The language of modern man is impoverished. The goal of his theology is, therefore, to realize a unity between human experience "and the religious symbols of ultimacy derived from its [theology's] explicit religious tradition."[18]

Gilkey is encouraged in this task by his belief that secular people are more religious and religious people more secular than they suppose themselves to be. In fact, "our secular life is saturated with religious elements, impoverished because they are inarticulated and so unexamined, but nevertheless, as we have argued, these sacred elements are as basic to our life amidst the profane as they were to any traditional religious culture."[19] In the latter stages of his argument Gilkey turns explicitly to Paul Tillich's theology of correlation: human experience creates the problems or questions, and religious inheritance provides a resource for the answers. Gilkey's hope for a more human future rests on the ability of interpretation to adumbrate a relationship between the depths of human experience and inherited religious symbols.

The anthropologies of these religious thinkers and the beliefs affecting character in the fiction discussed in this section offer a second deliniation of the human problem and its solution. Instead of incarceration within the distorting confines of a humanly created world this second belief sees the main illness of human life to be, or to arise from, cultural conflicts. Delivery through interpretation depends on the belief that the future is large enough to accommodate conflicting values. The marginal man, then, is the person who both suffers cultural conflicts and believes in their future resolution.

6

Jack Kerouac and Getting It Together

Many of the principal characters of Jack Kerouac's fiction are restless and mobile because they seek experiences of unity. They desire moments in which components of their lives are brought together into an intense, though impermanent, whole. The name for this moment or experience is "It." When Jack, in *Visions of Cody*, asks what "It" is, Cody replies, "We'll all know it when he hits it—there it is! he's got it—hear?—see everybody rock? It's the big moment of rapport all around that. . . ."[1] In their quest, Kerouac's characters expend great energy, travel long distances, and subject themselves to improvised or prescribed rituals and disciplines. And while there are leaders or teachers who help and friends who provide companionship along the way, the quest is finally carried on alone, "on foot, and in these little crepesole shoes."[2]

This desire for unity arises from a commitment to two conflicting cultures: a Catholic, French-Canadian past in Lowell, Massachusetts and contemporary America. The quest for "It" is primarily a search for a form of existence in which the resonance and rapport—which the ethnically and religiously unified community in Lowell provided—can be rediscovered later in relationships with artists and intellectuals.

On the Road, the most widely known of Kerouac's novels, typifies the quest. Leaving everything else behind, Sal Paradise and his companion Dean Moriarity travel to populated places where unity is likely to be found, such as San Francisco, Denver, and New Orleans. Their journey culminates in a trip to Mexico, a country which, because of its fecundity, promises to be a place "where we would finally learn ourselves among the Fellahin Indians of the world, the essential strain of the basic primitive, wailing humanity that stretches in a belt around the equatorial belly of the world. . . ."[3]

Visions of Cody, written soon after *On the Road*, also depicts this quest. However, while further travels to inviting locations are presented, the stress in this book is on certain disciplines which promise unity: concentration, provocation, and, most of all, rhythm. The right attitude and behavior are as crucial as an appropriate setting or suitable people.

The search for "It" continues in *The Dharma Bums*, Kerouac's most joyful narrative. Written after he had penned sadder tales, such as *Tristessa*,[4] it seems like a nostalgic recall of brighter days. In *The Dharma Bums* Ray Smith celebrates "the big moment of rapport" with the community of artists, intellectuals, and spiritual seekers after truth, especially with Japhy Ryder. This rapport is supported by nature; the work is replete with madonna and child images which describe Ray's attraction to the ground, the sea, the woods, the desert, and the mountains. Japhy, a product of fertile Oregon, is schooled in American Indian lore and is a devotee of Zen nature mysticism, especially of mountain-climbing sects. But contact with nature is less important than the experiences of rapport which arise between individuals of diverse backgrounds, tastes, and gifts.

Despite the moments of unity in *The Dharma Bums*, cultural conflict persists in Ray's life. Japhy rejects America and, at the end, leaves in order to be absorbed in the culture of Japanese Buddhism. Ray, although he admires Japhy, has deeper and continuing ties to this country. He travels not to Japan but back to his home in North Carolina. More democratic than Japhy, Ray strikes up friendships with bums and truckdrivers. Ray is less selective and ascetic than his friend, as their differences of opinion on eating in a restaurant and on drinking reveal. While Japhy responds to cultural conflict by dismissing the American, Western, or Christian side, Ray persists in looking forward to a future resolution.

From several of Kerouac's other novels we can determine why his characters expend so much energy on the quest for unity. The model for *communitas* is Lowell, Massachusetts, where Kerouac grew up. In the works to which we now turn, Lowell is a place where life is unified and spiritually full. "It," for his adult characters, is a sacramental reembodiment of the wholeness, now lost, which Lowell once provided.

Visions of Gerard presents Jack's older brother as an incarnation of spiritual gracefulness, whose orientation to heaven seems to elevate Lowell above ordinary America. This effect is enhanced by the way he dies and by the context of the Catholic Church, home, and school.

Lowell provided the adolescent Jack with a spiritual vision as well. His tutoring by Dr. Sax helps to articulate his obsessions with the past, death, women, and darkness, and he is led to a vision of evil and of the power of goodness to carry evil away. But *Doctor Sax: Faust Part Three* is not simply an anatomy of adolescent fear and forbidden desire. The mysterious is very much a part of the world in which the young boy, sensitive to transcendent power, lives.

Jack also had a great love in Lowell. In *Maggie Cassidy* he is loved by Lowell's most desirable young woman, "the mother or daughter of God." She is the best the town can offer its favorite son. Older than Jack, more passionate and experienced, quivering with domestic promise—she is too much for him. Maggie is not his only admirer, for young Jack is loved by other girls as well as by his friends and family; he holds a central position in a world rich with rapport. When he leaves the town to attend school in New York City, a permanent break occurs. He returns to claim his treasure, but Maggie is now beyond his grasp. Yet memories of Maggie and the community of which she is a part prevent Jack from being fully content with the loves and relationships to be found in adult American life.

Kerouac's first novel, *The Town and the City*, although it stands somewhat apart from his other works, indicates the radical break that this move involved. In the town, life was centered in the maternally dominated home and was integrated with its natural, social, and spiritual surroundings; in the city, there is isolation and scattering. While in the town there was rapport and spiritual intimacy, in the city there is individual frenzy and exploitation. The transition is from unity to disruption, from fullness to the threat of emptiness. In the city Peter looks back at the town as "the weather and veritable landscape of his soul."[5] There he had known "all the gravities and the glees and the wonders of life."[6] Now all is lost. Yet Peter turns, as did Kerouac, from nostalgia for an unavailable Eden to the present life as "a poor miserable disconnected fragment of something better, far greater. . . ."[7] He views the American population as a potential family, and, at the end of the book, he begins the quest for *communitas* through the rituals, now readily identified as Beat, which are central to *On The Road* and *The Dharma Bums*.

In another set of fictions the creative work of finding or establishing a community between disparate individuals becomes too difficult, and attention is given to finding unity in the self. For example, in *The Subterraneans* Jack is torn by conflicting loyalties, on the one hand to Mardou Fox and on the other to the group of frenzied artists and intellectuals. Mardou is more than a girlfriend; she is a maternal figure, "the first, the essential woman," who, because of her sex and her complex cultural makeup—half Negro and half Indian—is richly experienced in suffering. In contrast, the Subterraneans, given to drugs and orgies, lack content and stability. The irreconcilable conflict between these two interests turns Jack to tensions within himself and their consequences for his writing. He becomes uncertain about the subordination of experience to writing. Thus conflict becomes a matter of vocational and personal identity.

Tristessa also depicts disappointments, for Mexico lacks the spiritual promise it offered in *On The Road*. In the first part of the book, written more than a year before the second, Tristessa, though a victim, is still a point of light in the darkness of Mexico, and the ascetic narrator imagines her in the role of the Virgin. But in the second section, after the experiences narrated in *The Dharma Bums* and because of Tristessa's disintegration from morphine, she is inseparable from the depressing life around her. Moreover, Jack recognizes himself as a tourist in Mexico, a visitor to a hell that is permanent for its residents. His separation from Tristessa and her world is too great for him to overcome; disillusioned and distressed, he turns to private visions of completion and peace.

Desolation Angels continues to reveal the difficulty of finding *communitas* in adult American experience. The first of the two parts gives a very different rendering than does *The Dharma Bums* of the experience on Desolation Peak. Jack had expected to meet God there, but he came face-to-face, instead, with an emptiness in himself. Bored and eager to leave, he became sexually obsessed and failed to attain spiritual growth. The second part describes Jack's disenchantment with the artistic community which he struggled to create and maintain. Its members are preoccupied with themselves;

Irwin is struck by his new notoriety, and Raphael is self-centered, intolerant of human suffering, sexually predatory, and rude. This loss of the community is juxtaposed with Jack's memories of Gerard, of his mother, and of his youth. Despite total disillusionment, Jack continues to believe in an eternity "where all is restored again."[8]

Finally, in *Big Sur* the rapport with nature is undermined. Jack goes to Big Sur for rejuvenation after three years of a "drunken hopelessness." Despite some unfortunate delays, disappointments, and frights, he arrives and, living in a childlike way, begins to mend. But minor incidents unnerve him. These incidents led, he realizes, to temporary insanity because they all pointed to death: his claustrophobic terrors while drunk, the taste of the sea's "sick mortality," the death back home of his pet cat Tyke, and the visit to a hospitalized friend. Jack is disillusioned by what he has produced, not the "rucksack revolution" of joyous rapport that *The Dharma Bums* envisioned, but the Beat movement, its sham and shabbiness. Friendship with Cody and love with Billie provide some moments of respite, but rapport with nature is gone, and expectations previously held must be reduced.

These four fictions reveal the difficulty—perhaps the impossibility—of finding moments of unity which will fill the spiritual need created by the absence of Lowell. In several of the remaining works Kerouac presents his adjustment to not finding a substitute for the spiritual home he had known in his youth. That adjustment involves primarily an exchange of interpersonal relationships for individual wholeness.

Jack seeks personal integrity in *Satori in Paris* by making a pilgrimage to his ancestral home in Brittany. At first he becomes aware of the distance that has grown between himself and his origins. He has trouble getting there; he cannot locate the libraries and books he needs to trace his family; he misses the plane; he has trouble finding a room; and he feels homesick and lonely. A more important sign of this distance is his discovery that his pronunciation differs from that of the local people. Jack concludes that he and his family have kept the language pure in their North American French enclaves while the people in the old country have been exposed to the degenerating impact of history. He feels superior to his origins because of this purity.

Jack's heightened individuality, occasioned by his difficulty in reaching his destination and by his sense of superiority, brings on satori, or enlightenment, a moment which may have occurred in the taxi on the way to the airport. But the moment itself is not rendered. Such incidents, the story implies, are in life and not in books. The interpretation of cultural conflict can be found not in some place or community but in moments of internal peace.

A much darker version of this resolution is depicted in *Vanity of Duluoz: An Adventurous Education, 1935–46*. Covering much of the same period as *The Town and The City*, it gives a negative view of family relations, particularly between Jack and his father, and echoes the theme of Ecclesiastes that all is vanity. Jack's father pressed him toward achievements in football, education, and employment. Burdened by these expectations, Jack is released from them only by his father's death. His later experiences teach him that human existence is evil; the great sin is birth, and life is a prolonged sacrifice to death. Betrayals by football coaches, the war, the disorientation—these and similar moments reveal "the cruel nature of bestial creation."[9] Life is worth little more than "what it smells like down in the Bellevue Morgue."[10] A sharp turn is taken, therefore, from the task of interpreting the relation of Lowell to America to the task of finding moments of unity in the self; such moments do occur. By anticipating "endless interesting panoramas," Jack differs from Will Hubbard, who expects nothing, "his long gray face hopeless."[11] Rather than racing to pursue or struggling to create "It," Jack is reduced to awaiting brief moments that offer a reprieve from conflict and isolation.

Pic supports this resolution to the problem of not getting "It" together. The racial element in the book emphasizes cultural conflict and alienation in America. Despite this situation, Pic's brother Slim has such spiritual energy that all of the pain and disappoinment society inflicts cannot destroy his ability to celebrate little moments of joy.

Kerouac's fiction, then, is a study of the trials and strategies of the marginal man. The conflict of cultures, between the characters' French Canadian Catholic youth and contemporary America, does not compel them to reject either side but to affirm both, to create out of values drawn from each an identity and a way of life. This fusion primarily consists of trying to find in experience the same kind of resonance and rapport that was natural to life in Lowell. But the work is discouraging, and the conditions Jack encounters resist it. In the later books he settles for the rather passive capacity to recognize such moments of unity when they occur and to experience them privately.

Understanding and appreciating Kerouac's work depends, in large part, on the recognition of cultural conflict as a major spiritual dilemma in American experience. Like Walter Rauschenbusch and other American writers and thinkers, Kerouac attempted in his life and writing to make democratic and American those values found in a provincial and parochial setting. While this goal met with major reversals, it also led to success. When the quest for community is exchanged for a preoccupation with personal wholeness, the belief that conflict can be resolved and unity can be experienced continues to inform the writing. The energy and tenacity with which Kerouac addressed the problem of cultural conflict and the criticism to which he subjected its resolutions allow his work to be a significant example of the role and nature of this belief in contemporary American fiction.

7

Simplicity and Complexity in
Saul Bellow's Fiction

The characters in Saul Bellow's fiction often contrast secular urban America, which they view as morally and physically complex, with the simple and unified world of their Jewish youth. They do not fall victim to the weight and confusion of the present because of their search for or belief in the simple; and they are kept from nostalgia and escape to the past by their inextricable involvement with the complex. Life for them, then, lies between these alternatives. Many of these characters are late arrivals on the modern scene, and memories of their youth relate them to the premodern period. This situation adds an historical dimension to the cultural conflicts which determine their lives.

Bellow's characters do not resolve these tensions; achieved moments of unity are ephemeral. His characters, while they are engaging, gifted, and earnest men, are always, too, slightly inept or weak. Although their personal authority is compromised, they are granted stature by the cultural conflicts they suffer and by their persistent and energetic desire to resolve them.

Joseph, in *Dangling Man*, is caught between two worlds, the military, which he has not yet entered, and the civilian, which he must prepare to leave. He uses this interim to interpret the relationship between two other worlds, his past and the present. Retreating from his contacts in New York City, in the loneliness of a boardinghouse, Joseph pursues the question, "How should a good man live: what ought he to do?"[1] This question arises from the contrast between contemporary America and "his father's house and the few blocks adjacent," in Canada where he had been "allowed to encounter reality" and which instills in him yet "the hope of an impossible rejuvenation."[2] Because of the memory of his youth, Joseph's life in urban New York—his association with others, his job in a travel agency, his participation in various organizations, and his study of several figures of the Enlightenment—had become unsatisfying. While the present affords no resource for Joseph's spiritual needs, neither can he carry on the search in isolation from it, for being a good man requires contact with others. Further, the contemporary world has produced in him "craters of spirit," particularly the need "to know what we are and what we are for, to know our purpose, to seek grace."[3] Rather than reject the present and retreat into the seductive time suggested by Haydn's music, Joseph hopes for a new community formed between the past and present, a free and moral "colony of spirit."

Joseph's attempt to address the needs created by his adult experience with answers drawn from his youth seems to fail completely. He becomes increasingly irritable, dependent on his wife, and sensitive to a dwindling of his life's importance. At the end, he is ready for the military, ready to be "relieved of self-determination, freedom canceled."[4]

Similar tensions mark the life of Asa Leventhal in *The Victim*. During several months spent apart from his wife, Asa becomes increasingly aware of the complexity and sordidness of metropolitan life. Since his youth he has fought poverty and failure, and he now feels elevated about "the outcast, the overcome, the effaced, the ruined."[5] But he suffers from a sense of guilt and impending judgment because of the economic means by which he has removed himself from his past.

This distress is personified by Kirby Allbee. This former colleague awakens the guilt Asa feels for the damage he may have done to others in his own struggle toward success. Allbee claims that Asa, like all Jews, is not fully American and has exploited American society. This interpretation of Jewish attitudes toward American society, however bizarre, is taken seriously by Asa. His position is aggravated by uncertainty about his mental stability—his mother had died in an institution—and by the sickness and death of his nephew.

Asa can turn to no one for help. His friends are confident in their Jewish identity and worldly success; his brother has little to offer him; and his wife is absent. Asa stands alone, uncertain in his

Jewish-American position, aware of the ambiguities of economic security, sensitive to the needs of others around him, and threatened by the violence, dreariness, and moral lassitude of contemporary American life. These conflicts are not resolved.

The engaging narrator of *The Adventures of Augie March* also relates his attempts to deal with the complexities of urban society. His first problem is created by those who want to impose on him their own ways of handling life's uncertainties, who see the illegitimate Augie as raw material that needs shape if it is to have worth or durability. Grandma Lausch tries to suit him with ideals derived from old-world aristocracy. William Einhorn attempts to give him business sense. Mrs. Renling wants to groom him socially, and Simon tries to tutor him in the strategies of a profitable marriage. Augie responds to all of these attempts by associating with unpromising girls, accepting jobs with no future, and involving himself in less-than-legal schemes. Yet, unlike others, Augie does not protect himself by adopting some simple interpretation of reality or some program for gaining security. He is therefore aware of the nature of urban America: "many people together who beget nothing on one another."[6] When he viewed Chicago from his brother's window, a "terrible dumbness covered it, like a judgment that would never find its word."[7]

Augie responds to complexity by searching for a simplicity he associates with the sky. His first attempt to find it leads him to Mexico in the company of Thea Fenshal. But while Mexico offers sky and celestial associations, it becomes treacherous through the machinations of Thea and others. Later, by himself in Chicago, Augie gains awareness of "something infinitely mighty and great"[8] which will counterbalance the complexity. One morning—the first day of January—he looks at the blue sky above a Greek church and concludes that "The days have not changed, though the times have. The sailors who first saw America, that sweet sight, where the belly of the ocean had brought them, didn't see more beautiful color than this."[9] The sky encourages Augie, supporting his faith that "at any time life can come together again and man be rejuvenated . . . man himself, finite and taped as he is, can still come where the axial lines are."[10]

These axial lines represent Augie's affirmation that there exists within human life a simplicity and moral direction which correspond to the sky and stand in contrast to the confusion of daily existence. The axial lines are those directives in human relationships which undergird and validate them.

The affirmation of these verities does not cancel out the complexities of life. The economic crash affects Augie, too, and the war requires his enlistment. In addition, the axial lines cannot be given permanency: "You should never try to cook such butterflies in lard."[11] America is always there, complex, coercive, disappointing; but there, too, are the moments of contact with something permanently beautiful or true. Life is lived between these poles. As Augie concludes, "We are meant to be carried away by the complex and hear the simple like the far horn of Roland when he and Oliver are being wiped out by the Saracens."[12]

Another victim of the confusion of contemporary life is Tommy Wilhelm who at the beginning of *Sieze the Day* is already at an end; somewhat before this he made the last in a series of mistakes by giving his remaining funds to the untrustworthy Dr. Tamkin for speculative investments. Earlier, Tommy had ended his education for the sake of an acting career which would abort, and, because his estranged wife demands his money, he lacks financial resources as well as marketable skills. Tommy is a disappointment to his father, who requires success as a prerequisite for acceptance.

Tommy's father, the son of a dry goods merchant, rose to a respected and successful position as a physician. He is appalled by his son's lack of ambition and worldly wisdom. Consequently, Tommy, who resents his father's judgments, becomes involved with Dr. Tamkin less for financial than for personal reasons. Tamkin not only offers interesting insights into human nature and behavior, he also becomes for Tommy a substitute father.

Tamkin, although failing him financially, is able to help Tommy on this more spiritual level. He asserts that in each person there exist two souls, one real and one fabricated. If the fabricated or false soul tries to achieve supremacy, the real soul will assert itself, often in violence and even in murder or suicide. Tommy is suicidal; his true soul has been leading him to actions which subvert and destroy the intentions of the fabricated self. Tamkin urges Tommy to give his allegiance to the true soul primarily by living fully in every moment, by seizing the day.

The emergence of his true soul and his appreciation for the present come for Tommy through acts of honesty and a sense of community. He becomes increasingly direct with his wife and father. And, when he ultimately spills his heart's load of sorrow in the funeral parlor, he is no longer the man he was, of whom it could be said, "When it came to concealing his troubles, Tommy Wilhelm was not less capable than the next fellow."[13] His life has changed, and he is now free from the evasions and falsifications of the role he tried to fabricate for his father. Tommy has been able, however temporarily, to find a moment of peace.

Lack of paternal acceptance also aggravates the cultural and personal problems of the main character in *Henderson the Rain King*. Judging from his father's attitudes, Henderson believes that he should have died instead of his brother. This lack of legitimacy, combined with his sense that life has become "too complicated,"[14] create a thirst for reality. His constant cry is "*I want.*"[15]

Henderson seeks reality in spiritual and aesthetic quests. He studies the violin in the hope of communicating with his dead father: "This is me, Gene, on your violin, trying to reach you."[16] "*I wanted to raise myself into another world. My life and deeds were a prison.*"[17] Unsuccessful in finding reality and simplicity at home, he looks to a place outside of his culture. His quest takes him to Africa, where initially he finds everything "to be so simplified" and feels that he has "gone clean out of the world, for, as is common knowledge, the world is complex."[18] In addition to being "simplified and splendid,"[19] even biblical, Africa is associated by Henderson with his youth; as a boy he held a job in Ontario caring for an old bear named Smolah. In Africa he is willing to be drawn again to animal life; he achieves his greatest insights down on all fours and roaring like a lion.

By leaving the entanglement of contemporary American society for the liberating simplicity of Africa, however, Henderson seems only to exchange one kind of cultural estrangement for another. He is a bungling curiosity for the Africans he meets, and the many spiritual and literary associations with the place seem to keep him from, as much as lead him to, legitimacy and wholeness.

The humor of the book lies primarily in the undermining of Henderson's quest. He does not find the simplicity and reality for which he longs in Africa. Perhaps his position at the Arctic Circle near the end bridges the gap between America and Africa and grants a moment of peace.

Qualities found in Bellow's other characters—Joseph's dedication to goodness, Asa's sensitivity, Augie's spontaneity, Tommy Wilhelm's penchant for mistakes, and Henderson's energy—are all found in Bellow's most complicated character Moses E. Herzog. And the struggle between the cultural contraries of simplicity and complexity, past and present, moral and immoral, mark his experience as well.

Herzog gives up his academic post in New York City and moves with his new wife Madeleine and another couple to Ludeyville, Massachusetts in search of a simpler community and in order to find a separate, more intense, and heightened form of life. He makes this risky transition to gain, in addition, more respectability, "a solid footing in white Anglo-Saxon Protestant America."[20] Also important for the move is Herzog's memory of his father, who was always capable of boldness; it is with his inheritance that the new home is purchased. Finally, Herzog wants to regain the values of his youth, a time when there was "a wider range of human feelings than he had ever again been able to find."[21] This past reality makes him critical of the present and provides a model for the new life in Ludeyville.

Like other characters in Bellow's novels, Herzog views his youth as a time free from diseases that plague the modern age, which he characterizes as ". . . the mire of post-Renaissance, post-humanistic, post-Cartesian dissolution, next door to the void."[22] Urban life especially reveals a chaos which defies understanding and control: "He had to get out to the seashore where he could breathe."[23] The chaos includes both the physical, dense confusion of contemporary society and the morally shocking domestic cases he witnesses in court. His move to Ludeyville, then, constitutes an attempt to find a way of life free from the acids which mark modernity, rich in idiosyncrasies, and conducive to productive human relationships.

The plan is shattered by betrayal; Herzog had misjudged the motives and capacity of his wife and friend. At first he responds by escaping in anger and self-pity to the mothering sexuality of Ramona. He writes resentful and argumentative letters, most of them unposted. His trip to Chicago, however, is as much, and perhaps more, a retreat to his youth as it is an attempt to avenge himself. There his daughter June becomes for him "a reality" in contrast to the "bunk and paranoia" of his own attitudes and feelings. When Herzog hugs her against his "careworn, busted, germ-carrying"[24] self, he feels calmed.

The novel relates Herzog's ascent from consternation over the betrayal to peace of mind and the calm of simplicity. No longer writing letters, he feels released from the tyranny of his involvement, from the need to make frantic trips, and from the desire to justify himself. By himself in Ludeyville, he finds life whole again.

Lest we think that Herzog's achievement of peace between the complexity of his engagements with others and knowledge of modernity on the one hand and his ideal of a life resonant with personal integrity on the other is a model that should be emulated, we should note that Herzog, like Bellow's other characters, is always a bit off-center. His knowledge of modern history, his moral sensitivity, his appreciation of his personal past, and his good intentions all make him admirable, even likeable. But he is rash, easily deceived, and dependent on others, particularly on women and on his brother. The change in narrative point of view from first to third person seems to belittle him.[25] Herzog is not an authoritative figure, yet he remains a highly self-conscious suffering victim of cultural conflict who has responded energetically and sensitively to his problematic situation.

The central character of *Mr. Sammler's Planet* has a clear sense of cultural conflict not only because he comes late to contemporary America, as did Moses Herzog, but also because he is as old as the century and has been associated with its brightest as well as with its darkest moments. Before the war Sammler grew up in, and was nurtured by, a highly civilized atmosphere; the horrors of war presented a sharp contrast. The last part of his life—since his delivery in 1948 from a displaced persons camp—combines aspects of his former experiences; although New York City is brutal, Sammler tries to cultivate an elegant style.

From his observations of life in New York, Sammler develops a strong sense of ending. Confusion, despair, and moral chaos make the continuation of life doubtful. He disagrees with Professor Govinda Lal's solution of extending human life out into space, colonizing other planets. This answer only spreads the problem and postpones the crisis. He also disagrees with the attempts of several people to distinguish themselves from the confusion, to raise themselves above the mass. Margotte Arkin, his niece, deals with formulas instead of realities; she substitutes for the horrors of the concentration camps a phrase from Hannah Arendt. His daughter elevates her life by regarding her father as an unrecognized celebrity and by uring him to write about his friendship with H. G. Wells. Other people take an interest in Sammler, too, because they need something unusual by which to distinguish themselves. The student Pfeffer sees Sammler as a prophet from another world, and Elya Gruner treats him like a symbol of enlightened, old-world Jewry. These responses, which insist on personal distinction and special treatment, only add to the problem. Sammler also objects to nihilism as a response to the confusion of life. He sees around him a willingness to exalt madness, a celebration of sordidness and violence by people who lack his knowledge of what such forces can produce. The veneration of criminals and the interruption of his lecture by a student who appeals to the authority of excrement and the power of gonads mark a capitulation to attitudes capable of brutalizing life. Finally, he cannot accept the desire for power as an answer. Such responses as Angela's sexual paganism, Eisen's aesthetic ambitions, the pickpocket's pride in his masculine potency, and Wallace's lust for money are not viable.

For Sammler, escape to another planet, insistence on one's own uniqueness, thirst for destruction, and desire for power are inadequate or unfortunate responses to the decay and chaos of contemporary urban life. Yet, the confusion which threatens deprivation "because of volume, of mass, of the power to impart design"[26] cannot have the final say. Sammler feels the need for an answer, for order and simplicity. Without it "everything is poured so barbarously and recklessly into personal gesture."[27] Order of this kind is more important than love; perhaps it is love,[28] and Sammler's insistence on it is not another theory imposed on life. Rather, despite the complexity of human relations, there lies implicit in them, he believes, a natural moral structure. It is evident, he thinks, that Angela had injured her dying father and should ask forgiveness. It is also clear to him that Elya Gruner had tried to be a good man: ". . . through all the confusion and degraded clowning of this life through which we are speeding—he did meet the terms of his contract. The terms which, in his inmost heart, each man knows."[29] For Sammler, within the complexity of life exist simple lines of order which, if followed, could create "justice on this planet."[30]

For Charlie Citrine in *Humboldt's Gift* simplicity is less an underlying moral structure in human relationships than a spiritual reality outside of this life. Meditating on a passage from Baudelaire, Charlie says, "real life flowed between *here* and *there*."[31] *Here* is primarily Chicago, characterized by his entanglements with friends like Cantabile and his legal battles with his estranged wife Denise. *There* is a range of things: states of clarity achieved in meditation, the realm of the dead, Spain, and his youth. *Here* is where his brother Julius, his friend Cantabile, and his mistress Renata live. Charlie acknowledges the need for constant exposure to their values. *There*, though, is where his heart is. He approaches this other world through meditation and an appreciation for the inner life. These disciplines are intended to counteract the consequences of the last three centuries during which a "lack of a personal connection with the external world"[32] has become pervasive. Boredom is a symptom of the situation, and Charlie is conducting a full-scale study of boredom in contemporary life.

There is also the realm of the dead, and chief among its inhabitants is Humboldt. A poet who suffered keenly the lack of culture in America and who died in the squalor of a New York City tenement, Humboldt in death is more alive to Charlie than ever before. Humboldt believed that poetry recalled an "original world, a homeworld, which was lost."[33] This poetic world, which Humboldt now inhabits, promises Charlie satisfaction for the "longing, the swelling heart, the tearing eagerness of the deserted, the painful keenness or infinitizing of an unidentified need."[34]

Spain also stands over *there*. It is a kind of Ellis Island for the alternative world because it has the remnants of a culture and because of its deep and tangled spiritual history. "There was significant space" in Spain.[35]

Although his past is marked by its own ambiguities, Charlie draws on his youth for much of what constitutes or points to *there*. He is an expert on his past. Indeed, Julius compares Charlie's memory with that of their grandfather, who knew the Babylonian Talmud by heart. From the past, which he views as a time of emotional intimacy, Charlie derives his desire for goodness.[36] He tells Naomi Lutz, his childhood sweetheart, that if they had married his life would have been free from the distortions it has suffered. His youth was a time when mind and culture, ideal and actuality, symbol and fact were unified. Like several of Bellow's characters, Charlie associates his youth with a premodern period:

. . . and there was the insignificant Picasso sculpture with its struts and its sheet metal, no wings, no victory, only a token, a reminder, only the idea of a work of art. Very similar, I thought, to other ideas or reminders by which we lived—no more apples but the idea, the pomologist's reconstruction of what an apple once was, no more ice cream but the idea. The recollection of something delicious made of substitutes, of starch, glucose, and other chemicals, no more sex but the idea or reminiscence of that, and so with love, belief, thought, and so on.[37]

There forms a contrary to the entanglements, depletions, and brutality of contemporary life. It is a realm of simplicity, wholeness, and peace.

When the two realms are separated, many forget the existence of *there* or despair of its reality: "The weight of the sense world is too heavy for some people and getting heavier all the time."[38] Conversely, a few, like Humboldt, seem almost fully absorbed with the *there*. But for Charlie, as for the other main characters in the Bellow corpus, life is a matter of affirming both. As Charlie puts it, life needs both a "vivid actuality" and a "symbolic clarity."[39] Their separation is the problem to which the imagination, "that savior faculty,"[40] must respond. The poet, states Renata, quoting Charlie's words back to him "is the arbiter of the diverse."[41] He is the one who points out the possibility of a whole life, who creates a "relationship between *here* and *there*."[42]

Saul Bellow's heavy investment in character, then, is a function of his preoccupation with cultural conflict. His characters are men who identify themselves with two conflicting worlds. Although these worlds are described and experienced in varying ways, the terms "simplicity" and "complexity" aptly summarize the conflict. The problem cannot be solved by rejecting one world for the sake of the other. The complex, typified by experience in contemporary urban America, is related to the simpler life of a premodern world as question is to answer. Bellow's characters are shaped by a question we also found in the work of Langdon Gilkey: How can the deficiencies and evils of the contemporary world be interpreted by resources and insights brought from the past? Answers are tentative and elusive, and the question must be posed continuously.

83

8

Tragic Conflict in Ken Kesey's
Novels

As the works of Kerouac and Bellow indicate, cultural conflict, while it may begin as ethnic distinctiveness in relation to American society, easily assumes wider dimensions. For Kerouac, cultural conflict leads to questions of personal identity and problems of communal relationships. For Bellow the tension between two worlds— secular and Jewish, present and past, external and internal—raises the larger problem of the relation of raw experience to inherited or traditional meaning and symbol. Cultural conflict leads to tensions and ambiguities which seem inherent to human life. In other words, within the concept of cultural conflict lies the potential for a tragic vision. This potential is realized in the fiction of Ken Kesey. Although ethnic considerations are present in his novels, major conflicts arise when differing people represent human life at war with itself. Thus, Kesey's characters reflect Reinhold Niebuhr's point that historical, cultural, and intellectual tensions attach themselves to, or are symptoms of, ambiguities constitutive of human life itself.

The move from cultural conflict to tragedy creates the epic scope of Kesey's two novels. In *One Flew Over The Cuckoo's Nest* he achieves breadth by allowing all of the elements of narrative to have a significant role. The ward, a setting which is both a particular place and a microcosm of American society, is a major source of the work's power and meaning. The classical three-part plot moves from the conflict between McMurphy and Big Nurse, through the passion of their struggle, to both the reversal of McMurphy's fortunes and the recognition of the results of his efforts. The tone adds significance because the principal fruit of McMurphy's campaign is the ability it releases in the Chief to relate what occurred. But, however important these other elements are to the narrative, character is preeminent.

Kesey uses character to reveal cultural antagonisms and tragic conflicts in human life. For example, the experiences of the Chief represent the destructively unfortunate way in which Americans tend to address cultural conflict. The Whites he encountered as a youth had no interest in the qualities of Indian culture and no appreciation of its legitimate conflicts with their own. The majority culture is disdainful toward, and destructive of, individuals who, for whatever reason, differ from it. The Chief, ignored by white people, absorbed this state of noncommunication by feigning deaf-muteness. A separation of schizophrenic and paranoid dimensions sets in between himself and the white culture around him.

Drawing on the experiences of his youth, the Chief associates the psychiatric ward, which he calls a "combine," with American society. Both resent difference and handle it by reducing the size of the nonconforming, offending party. The Chief makes two judgments concerning this approach to cultural conflict. The first is that it is violent both in effect and in cause. Those who respond to difference in this manner have themselves been victims of social violence. The black attendants are assailants because they have suffered brutal racist acts. The Big Nurse served in the army, and she suffers, we may conclude from the comments of the Japanese nurse, society's prejudice against unmarried women. The Chief's second observation is that society is primarily maternal. This at first seems anomalous; generally, as in Kerouac's fiction, the maternal figure is associated with nature and the paternal with society. But the Chief recalls how his strong and noble father was reduced by his white mother, a situation which corresponds to the attitudes of several patients toward their wives and mothers. He remembers, also, pulling his blanket over his head, disturbed because the stars were unable to maintain their brightness in the presence of the dominating, maternal moon. Furthermore, the ward is under the control of Big Nurse, whose principal physical characteristic is her ample bosom. Her presence suggests that society is a terrible mother who enslaves her children by making them dependent upon her at the price of their own individual energy. Rather than nurture and release, the terrible mother subjects and threatens with rejection.

Despite the heavy repression exerted by the atmosphere, there is a significant temporal movement in the narrative. In the first section, which ends with the World Series dispute, the problematic situation is revealed. Unsocialized, energetic, and self-interested, McMurphy stands as the social contrary and inevitable antagonist to Big Nurse. The lines are quickly drawn as the two recognize one another as threats. McMurphy attempts to beat Big Nurse at her own game, bringing the patients under his control and imagining them into a different world.

In the second part the real struggle begins, for McMurphy learns the stakes. He alone among his fellows on the ward has been committed, and his only hope for release is through cooperation. At first, naturally self-interested, he keeps in line. But after Cheswick's suicide—for which he feels partially responsible—and after he discovers the plight of the epileptics, witnesses Harding's intimidation by his wife, and recognizes that it is not Big Nurse but the entire system that opposes him, McMurphy rises to the challenge despite its personal cost. His major efforts are the fishing trip and the ward party. Contact during the trip with the sea and air, his challenge to the others that they should imagine themselves into another story, and the laughter and pranks that mark the outing have a therapeutic effect on the patients. But as the Chief recognizes, the effort tires McMurphy. In addition, the party for Billy Babbitt is preceded by determined attempts on the part of Big Nurse to undermine McMurphy and, more immediately, by the brawl with the attendants. Consequently, the reversals which characterize the third part of the plot are anticipated in the second.

The denuding of Big Nurse and the lobotomizing of McMurphy end the conflict and reveal that McMurphy had no real chance of winning. But the plot is not entirely pathetic. The effects of McMurphy's acts are seen in the changes the other patients, particularly the Chief, undergo. Not only does he leave the ward and reveal himself able to tell the story, the Chief is also able to transcend his own cultural conflict and to see the relation between McMurphy and Big Nurse as tragic.

The nature of the conflict implies that the two characters do not represent the extremes of good and evil. Of course, the position of Big Nurse is amplified because it is supported by American society.

Furthermore, unlike McMurphy, she does not change in the course of the plot. Although Big Nurse appears the more sinister from the outset, she and McMurphy represent conflicting kinds of cultural loyalty—to spontaneity and to discipline, to the self and to the group, to immediate reward and to sublimation, to energy and to order. While the reader tends to side with the underdog McMurphy, especially since the Chief favors him, the immediate problem of America's intolerance of individuality and ethnic distinctiveness should not conceal the more basic problem revealed by the narrative. Tragic antagonisms are constitutive of human life. This situation, when not recognized, is aggravated by the tendency of people to solve conflicts by identifying with one side and by ignoring or attacking the other.

The move from cultural to tragic conflicts is even clearer in *Sometimes a Great Notion.* The shift is enhanced by the parallels drawn in the work between conflicts in the lives of its characters and moments in tragic literature, especially classical and Shakespearean. The most noticeable cultural conflict in this second novel is that between individual and corporate interests. Hank Stamper, with the support of his father Henry, resists the logging union and its appeals to a common good by affirming, in opposition, the primacy of individual freedom. The people of the town, those woodsmen interested in the union, insist, "No, sir, no man is a goddam island."[1] For Hank it is a different matter: "But if somebody— Biggy Newton or the Woodsworker's Union or anybody—gets into it with *me*, then I'm for *me!*"[2] There is a natural relationship between the parties in this struggle: they have the same difficult lot. The people of the town understand and respect the Stampers, even admire them, but the townspeople's collective interests constitute a valid point of view which conflicts with the Stampers' defiant individuality.

A second tragic conflict—one reminiscent of the parable of the prodigal son—exists between the elder and the younger half brothers, Hank and Leland. Hank has remained in his father's home in Oregon working hard in the family business while Leland has gone East, attended college, developed an interest in poetry, and participated in the drug culture. Hank is rugged, a man of action rather than words, while Leland is oriented to women, sensitive, cerebral, and dependent. Their conflict, echoed in the rift between Jonathan Draeger and Floyd Evenwrite, arises from more than personality differences or even sibling rivalry. The brothers embody two kinds of cultural orientation. Furthermore, they have a mutual respect. Hank encourages Leland to talk with Vivian about books, and Leland agrees to go hunting with Hank. They learn from one another as partners in a tension-ridden relationship. Finally, their complementary relation can be seen in the love Vivian has for them both. Yet they clash, with tragic consequences, like two ways of life or two sets of values.

A conflict between personal action and the larger historical context of which the individual actor cannot be fully aware is also depicted in this novel. Each character always acts in at least partial ignorance of the entire situation. The resulting tragic outcome can be seen in the unnecessary and unwarranted injuries the characters cause one another. Hank is too preoccupied with his work to realize that Leland's association with Vivian will feed a neglected side of her life. Leland does not know when he goes to the house to have sex with Vivian that his older brother is already down, already hurt. What is more important, Leland, because he thought that his mother had been seduced by Hank, has nurtured a decade of hate and a desire for revenge against his brother. He only later learns that it was his mother who had seduced Hank. More generally, the tragic consequences arising out of the conflicts between individual actions and larger contexts are revealed in the conditioning of people by their particular backgrounds. As Vivian tells Draeger, " 'You could never understand it all. You just want a reason, two or three reasons. Where there are reasons going back two or three hundred years.' "[3] Similarly, Floyd Evenwrite works on behalf of the union because of the influence his father had on him. Conflicts arise, then, between individual actions and larger temporal contexts and between characters and their own histories.

A final area of tragic conflict is depicted in the relation of the Stampers to nature. What makes these men bigger than their counterparts—like Teddy the barkeeper, Willard Eggleston, and even the toughs who intimidate Leland—is that they live between the river and the mountains and wrestle with nature's mightiest sons, the trees. The negative quality of this relationship is underscored by the fall season. The Stampers resent nature: "You need to get in there with some machines an' tear hell out of it,"[4] says Henry, and Hank has a "grudge match" with the river, which continuously encroaches on their land.

The Stampers face tensions which are more than cultural. The cultural conflicts in the novel yield to tensions which are tragic because they pit values against one another: the individual and the group, the person and history, human will and nature.

Kesey does not leave us, however, with the pathos of human life divided against itself; in his writing there is belief in the power of imagination to transcend a conflict and to interpret it in relation to the larger human situation. Chief Bromden, although he identifies most fully with McMurphy, is able to depict all parties involved. His experience of the destructive way in which Americans address cultural conflict does not force him to respond similarly. The implied author of *Sometimes a Great Notion* ranges widely in the world he presents, indicating that the characters and their conflicts are parts of a larger, unified whole which the imagination can perceive and impart. This ability to transcend one's own position and to see the validity of opposing stances is an answer to the threat to moral and spiritual integrity posed by conflicts which are culturally derived or which characterize the structure of human life.

PART THREE

PRIESTS OF THE POSSIBLE

9

Incompleteness and Transcendence

The third belief shaping character in American fiction is suggested by Irving Howe, who notes that we expect our writers to "establish a realm of values at a distance from the setting of actual life, thereby becoming priests of the possible in a world of shrinking possibilities." These dissociated values are seen Howe continues "not so much in terms of an improvement or reordering of the social structure, but as a leap beyond society—a wistful ballet of transcendence."[1] The third belief deals, then, not with man's relation to the larger context of the natural, subhuman, or preconscious world of which he is a part nor with the conflicts between cultures and within human nature; rather, it deals with the need—created by the incompleteness or confusion of experience—for imagined, projected, or intuited forms of transcendent coherence and wholeness.

That this third belief is deeply embedded in the American tradition is evinced by Richard Poirier, who concludes that the major distinction to be made in American fiction is not between the novel and the romance (as Richard Chase asserts in *The American Novel and Its Tradition*); rather, Poirier distinguishes between fictions in which characters find no recourse from the brute particulars of their experience and those in which the characters, by acts of imagination or belief, find alternative worlds which transcend their environments and which they are able to entertain.[2]

This belief seems consistent with a major religious heritage granted with the settling of America, especially the Calvinist emphasis on divine transcendence which placed people's hope for completion beyond the realm of their terrestial experience. Models of fulfillment, whether corporate, as in the figure of the righteous city, or personal, as in biblical types, countered any notion that the wholeness for which people thirst and the ambiguities which torment life can be granted or resolved by history. The experiment of establishing a righteous community, which Perry Miller discusses in his *Errand Into the Wilderness*, reveals that the Puritans perceived their separation from the accumulations of culture not as a return to natural vitalities but as an opportunity more closely to imitate an ideal. John Lynen, in his *Design of the Present*, shows how deeply the American literary tradition imbibed the Puritan tendency to reduce life to a transaction between the present and the eternal, the individual and the universal.

A Calvinist of the sort Perry Miller describes would, however, be uncomfortable with the status of the transcendent in this third belief. The Calvinist insistence on divine sovereignty and on the responsibility of the Christian to glorify God is more theocentric than the belief allows. The interest in transcendence which we shall observe in the formation of character in American fiction cannot be taken as directly related to these Calvinist emphases. A major transition to the anthropocentrism of the belief is provided by Deism and Idealism in American culture. A spokesman for Deism like Tom Paine or of Idealism like Emerson would begin not with the power or primacy of God but with natural and human needs and possibilities. The orientation of this belief is not a vague form of Calvinist theocentrism; rather, it has its own integrity and sources, and it should be related to the two beliefs we examined earlier.

In our century the need for transcendent forms of completion and coherence is aggravated by a general uneasiness with experience which is, as Nathan A. Scott states, "without organic order, presided over by a philosophical and religious pluralism of the most extreme sort."[3] In an increasingly disordered and unsatisfying world, the need for transcendent wholes becomes more urgent. At the same time, however, they are more tentative, private, and improvised. Robert Scholes, whose book *The Fabulators* deals with fiction strongly influenced by this belief, notes that these forms may not be symbols of some higher program actually believed in or hoped for but "an allegory of the mind of man with its rage for an order superior to that of nature."[4] Whether toward transcendent wholes spiritually affirmed or metaphysically secured, toward cosmological images derived from subjective experiences,[5] or toward completion and coherence as a potential in and for imagination or language[6]— the move from a disordered, disappointing, and even evil world to a compensating and unifying imagined alternative is one of the three main beliefs of man's spiritual life affecting the formation of characters in American fiction.

Emerson is a central figure for the articulation of this belief; as Lewis Mumford puts it, "he made us conscious of those qualities native to the soil that distinguishes it from the literature of other nations."[7] Tony Tanner remarks that "certain novel attitudes and predilections which recur in many American writers seem to emerge articulated in Emerson's work for the first time."[8] Emerson, Tanner argues, epitomizes a particular current of American spiritual experience and reflection which continues to influence American writing today.

Nature, Emerson says in his early essay on the subject, leads to spirit. It does so first by confronting the beholder as a contrary, as the "Not-me." By employing Aristotle's four causes, Emerson proceeds to describe the uses of nature which lead to its final cause, to provide man a spiritual discipline. The experience of contrariety leads to wholeness because of spirit by which both man and nature are enfolded. This spirit is, for Emerson, transcendent and eternal.[9]

The stress of Emerson's thought is on the integrity or wholeness of individual human life, as "The Divinity Class Address of 1838" readily reveals. However, he does not confine the need for transcendence to individuals. Life is also, for Emerson, a pilgrimage toward a celestial city, as Michael Cowan reveals.[10] There is no resolution in history for the tensions which mark society: power and form, necessity and freedom, matter and spirit, individual and universal. These conflicts point beyond themselves to a transcendent unity.

Finally, language is related to the need and possibility for transcendence. Kenneth Burke argues, for example, that for Emerson language is a link between disparate realms. Burke calls this use of language "pontification," or bridge building, because it suggests movement from the incomplete to the whole, from nature to spirit.[11]

Priest of the possible, to use Howe's phrase, or bridge builder, to use Burke's—Emerson presides over those impulses in American writing that direct attention to the possibility of transcendent completion and coherence. Belief of this sort is found to underlie major and influential American narratives as well as religious and theological anthropologies.

Characters in the fiction of Edgar Allan Poe tend to move from an incomplete world of appearance to a coherent and attractive spiritual reality behind it. By a *via negativa*, the everyday world is stripped away or dissolved, and characters are brought over thresholds to places where matters are not as they normally expect them to be.

Many of Poe's characters actively engage in disciplines which will allow them passage over these thresholds. The narrator of "Berenice," for example, is capable of riveting his attention on the minute details of an object. This concentration negates his normal context, and new possibilities arise. The narrator of "Ligeia" is so obsessed by his dead wife that his second wife becomes transparent. In tales such as "William Wilson," transactions with a world other and more real than the world of appearance are forced on the characters against their will or without their expectation. In others exhaustion, illness, or drugs cause susceptibility to radical changes in orientation; the narrator of "The Man of the Crowd," for example, is in a state of transition because of his recent return to health. For still other characters, access to an alternate world is granted by their lack of psychological balance; the narrator of "Eleonora" states that "the question is not yet settled, whether madness is or is not the loftiest intelligence—whether much that is glorious—whether all that is profound—does not spring from disease of thought—from *moods* of mind exalted at the expense of the general intellect."[12] Such a mad or imbalanced man is Prince Prospero, who sequesters himself and his guests in an enclosed and labyrinthine hall to escape death only to confront it more strikingly at the end.

Mention of "The Masque of the Red Death" reminds us that setting also creates the threshold situation. The narrator of "The Fall of the House of Usher," for example, finds himself in the vestibule of an uncanny world that leads to his apocalyptic vision. The principal character of "The Pit and the Pendulum" is in a nightmarish state which induces a total loss of his hold on the familiar. This process of unnerving, John Lynen interestingly compares to the effects created by Jonathan Edwards's famous sermon "Sinners in the Hands of an Angry God," in which the plight of mankind is described with increasing intensity.[13]

Poe explores common moments of experience in which access to a supranormal world seems granted. In "Marginalia" he develops the possibilities in the transition between wakefulness and sleep. Another moment in which hold on the normal world is undercut Poe calls the tendency toward perversity. "The Imp of the Perverse" and "The Black Cat" treat unmotivated evil acts which break down the familiar connections by which the world of appearances is sustained. Rents in the fabric of time also provide unexpected revelations. For example, the setting of "The Cask of Amontillado" between carnival and Lent provides the sudden transition from the comic to the deadly which is repeated in the plot. Finally, as in "Hop-Frog," Poe deals with the sudden transfer of mood, the exchange of horseplay for treachery, which reveals the unrecognized thinness of the line between the two. By means of these strategies, Poe leads the reader to thresholds of another world.[14]

These interests can also be seen in the ratiocinative tales, in his literary criticism and theory, and in *Eureka*. The work of our detective friend Dupin is to intuit from the welter of distracting details the true situation, the real plot. This kind of mental discipline looks beyond the confusion of things as they appear to the simple and unitary reality behind them. The detective, the theorist, the poet, and the metaphysician of *Eureka* press towards this true vision for, as one of Poe's critics puts it, "all forms and all created matter conform to the law of 'simplicity' or the law of unity from which everything has come and to which everything will inevitably return."[15] The simpler matters are more original and closer to God's mind. The disciplines inherent in Poe's work, then, are attempts to overcome relations to a superficial, derivative, and disunified world and to return to the simplicity of God's ideas. As he says toward the end of *Eureka*:

> With this understanding, I now assert that an intuition altogether irresistible, although inexpressible, forces me to the conclusion that what God originally created—that that Matter which, by dint of His

Volition, He first made from His Spirit, or from Nihility, *could* have been nothing but Matter in its utmost conceivable state of—what?—of *Simplicity*.[16]

The destiny of superior intelligence is to pursue this simplicity with all the urgency of monomania.

Poe's beliefs are most full actualized in *The Narrative of Arthur Gordon Pym*. Pym moves from ordinary associations and expectations through experiences of increasing severity which cut his cultural ties. His divestment is a movement toward a less civilized state, and it results in his decreasing confidence in his own ability to control his life. At the end he is ready for an exit from this world. This novel is Poe's boldest and most extended rendering of the process of gaining egress from this world.

The spiritual discipline underlying Thoreau's *Walden* is, in part, one of divestment as well. However, *Walden* affirms a relation between an individual and his world that is not found in the apocalyptic and death-obsessed fiction of Edgar Allan Poe.

The discipline of simplifying which Thoreau advocated through homilies, parables, and proverbs begins with an exclusion from life of all nonessential matters. This divestment permits a more accurate alignment with a nature which lies behind society and is "unprofaned." Only in contact with nature can the individual satisfy his need to know if life is mean or sublime.

Rather than end here, however, Thoreau's spiritual discipline also overcomes nature. Free from society, a person can recognize his savage instincts; the process of spiritual growth grants the assurance "that the animal is dying out of him day by day." "Nature is hard to overcome, but she must be overcome."[17] Unlike man, nature does not have an eternal dimension; the pond has a bottom: "The amount of it is, the imagination, give it the least license, dives deeper and soars higher than Nature goes."[18] This means that mythic and ritualistic interpretations of *Walden*, although satisfying to a degree, misplace the emphasis, for while nature is unprofaned and while *Walden* itself is ordered by a natural cycle of death and rebirth, the capacity of the human spirit to be renewed and to seek the eternal gives nature its meaning. Surely the "universe is wider than our views of it,"[19] but the human spirit is wider yet. This point is neglected by those who explore the reaches of the oceans but leave uncharted the "continents and seas in the moral world, to which every man is an isthmus or an inlet."[20]

The resulting self-image of Thoreau is complex. First, he is firmly footed in nature, a person of stability who neither acts out of anxiety nor is influenced by the opinions of others. Second, catholic in his interests, he is an astute observer of human life who appreciates the insights of all people and not just those of "our church." Finally, he is oriented to moments of spiritual completion. While all three of these components are important for *Walden*, the third, the transcendent orientation, is the dominant.

The naturalism of *The Red Badge of Courage* distinguishes Stephen Crane's writing from the spiritual interests and disciplines of Poe and Thoreau. Crane's naturalism, however, is primarily a method of treating character rather than a belief. He places the individual in situations of stress in order to reveal human nature. The testing reveals that will yields to the impulse to survive and intellect is replaced by, or dissolved into, the imagination—a world of models, memories, and hopes which compensates for or complements the circumstances that threaten life.

Henry Fleming lives in two worlds which are separate but which influence one another: the world of bitter fact and the fairly elaborate realm of his ideals, expectations, and memories. This fundamental human structure, revealed under stress, is supported in the novel by the image of the sun's relation to the earth and by the shifts made from Henry's awareness to views of him, so to speak, from above.

It is clear from the outset that Henry has an active imagination. He is a fairly reclusive, reflective person whose transactions are primarily with images of possibilities. This orientation isolates him from, and in his own mind elevates him above, the others, even officers who, like the lieutenant, "had no appreciation of fine minds."[21]

Henry is also susceptible to the impact of circumstances. In the initial battle he feels reduced: "He became not a man but a member."[22] In the first part of the story there is no release from this tormenting dissociation of imagination from circumstances. The road to nature leads to the chapel of death; Jim's demise, the questions of the tattered man, and the procession of the gallant leave Henry with no human companions.

The blow on the head—along with the sense of alienation from nature and his comrades—is accompanied by a revival of Henry's imaginative life. He remembers vividly swimming nude with boyhood friends and his mother's spread table. His imagination allows the actions of the day before to grant him confidence: "And furthermore, how could they kill him who was the chosen of gods and doomed to greatness?"[23]

His return to the front is the consequence of this imaginative life, and his heroic action arises from the maternal associations with the flag which his mind creates. Identified with this image, as he apparently was not identified with the male images of heroism at the beginning of the story, he becomes "savage, religion-mad." "It was a woman, red and white, hating and loving, that called him with the voice of his hopes."[24] Reconstituted by this association with an inclusive feminine image, Henry turns with a "lover's thirst to images of tranquil skies, fresh meadows, cool brooks—an existence of soft and eternal peace."[25]

The story moves, then, from Henry's "eternal debate" between impulse and ideal, through both the domination of his heroic models by his instinct to survive and his alienation from nature and comrades, to the absorption of desire by a maternal figure which his own mind creates. At the end Henry is a reborn child of the imagination, turning toward new, transcendent possibilities.

With these writers from the American narrative tradition stand a number of our contemporaries who are no less oriented to transcendent coherence and completion. Vladimir Nabokov, for example, although he cannot be taken as American in any direct way, gives us characters formed by this belief. An admirer of Edgar Allan Poe and an influence on Thomas Pynchon, Nabokov creates fictive worlds oriented to possibilities which lie in the realm of memory, fantasy, and death. These worlds are more permanent and powerful for his characters than accidental and incidental circumstances which easily dissolve into, or are transparent to, something more real. Art does not imitate daily experience for Nabokov; daily experience is secondary to art. And the power of language, like the power of memory, defeats time and suggests possible patterns. In addition, Nabokov is intensely interested in games, particularly chess, as *The Defense* reveals, and in the camera, as we can see in

Laughter in the Dark. Even in the straightforward novel *Pnin*, Nabokov creates a character atuned, to use his phrase, to a "spiritual time." He is so directed because in ordinary time his boyhood sweetheart Mira, that "graceful, fragile, tender young woman with those eyes, that smile, those gardens and snows in the background, had been brought in a cattle car to an extermination camp. . . ."[26] For Nabokov, the language of fiction serves, in Burke's words, a pontificating function, leading the imagination of the reader to forms of coherence and completion that transcend ordinary experience.

A similar orientation shapes other characters in contemporary American fiction. For Flannery O'Connor, the violence of human experience is resolved by the reality of an eschatological form, such as the vision granted to Francis Tarwater at the end of *The Violent Bear It Away*. For the younger Glass children in the stories of J. D. Salinger, Seymour is a model of spiritual simplicity and completeness. And in Robert Coover's *The Universal Baseball Association* Henry Waugh dissociates himself from daily contacts and becomes absorbed entirely into the world of the baseball game he himself has created. Moreover, the interest expressed by Nabakov, Coover, and other contemporary writers in games indicates an orientation to images of coherence and completion that transcend the uncertain and unconnected particulars of ordinary life.[27]

Characters shaped by this third belief experience neither imprisonment in worlds of their own making from which they must be released to make contact with natural forces nor situations of cultural conflict which must be resolved; rather, the plight of the individual is the incomplete or incoherent quality of experience, a need which compels characters to imagine worlds which offer the possibility of transcendent wholeness.

Representative religious thinkers who utilize this belief for their anthropologies reveal that this way of construing human need and its fulfillment is pervasive in our culture. Like the writers of fiction studied in this chapter, these theologians understand human experience as incoherent or incomplete and as driving the individual to seek relief in transcendent unity.

In Josiah Royce's *The Problem of Christianity*, the act of interpretation must address the problem of a broken world, distinguished by the separation of the modern mind from the Christian tradition. This work *can* go on because the created whole, which is the goal and the product of interpretation, precedes us. Genuine interpretation, whenever it occurs, is evidence of the "Spirit of the Community of Interpretation," which is an inclusive, mainly hidden spiritual force producing concord.

Interpretation is, for Royce, a proper response to all instances of fragmentation. For example, the tension between the individual and collective aspects of human life can degenerate into hostility and alienation, into individual*ism* and collectiv*ism*. In order to avoid this danger, loyalty to the community of interpretation is needed. In this ideal community individuals are a part of a whole without loss of their unique characteristics. Thus, more than the sum of its individual members, the community is a spiritual reality that unifies life by granting moments of wholeness and peace.

For H. Richard Niebuhr, a thinker heavily influenced by Royce, the value of human life depends on relationships of trust and commitment. Yet while everyone has such relationships, most people are fragmented because they place their faith in many different things. For example, the individual trusts and is committed to his work, his family, his possessions, and his community. The situation becomes aggravated when these loyalties conflict. The confusion that results from this array of separated values is characteristic of the form of faith termed by Niebuhr, polytheism.

Some try to solve the problem of fragmentation by making one of these relationships primary. So, for example, a person will place loyalty to his country or to some ideal above every other relationship and subject the others to it. Rather than many "gods," then, he has one from among them. Niebuhr calls this kind of commitment henotheism. Its solution to fragmentation is unsatisfactory because such an object of faith can neither be ultimate nor sustain the commitment entrusted to it.

Niebuhr argues that the inadequacies of polytheism and henotheism can only be overcome by monotheism, loyalty to that which transcends all values and is their source. With this solution the individual can return to his world and find it unified, for the source of all values grants meaning to particulars in the world as well: "Here is the basis then not only of a transformed ethics, founded on the recognition that whatever is, is good, but of transformed piety or religion, founded on the realization that every being is holy."[28] For Niebuhr, the incoherence and incompleteness of life arise from our conflicting values. The experience of fragmentation drives us to transcend these many relationships through faith in a source of all value which lies outside our world.

When Shubert Ogden says that belief in God is unavoidable, he is not emphasizing the logical coerciveness of such acceptance, although such argumentation is intrinsic to his method; nor does he mean that belief is required by a metaphysical description of the structure of our world, although there is a strongly metaphysical and speculative quality to his thought. Neither does he suggest that belief in God is forced upon us by our experience, although the empirical and existential characteristics of his method are also clear. Rather, for Ogden—in a way reminiscent of William James—belief in God is necessary because it allows us to be at home in the universe. Ogden's statement that "for the secular man of today, as surely as for any other man, faith in God cannot but be real because it is in the final analysis unavoidable,"[29] refers to something constitutive or prior to personal existence. Belief in God allows life to be complete.

Theology for Ogden is primarily anthropology, since a theology is "mythological and untenable when it denies that statements about God may be interpreted as statements about man."[30] Theological propositions "must be at least implicitly about man and his possibilities of self-understanding if they are not to be incredible and irrelevant."[31] Although the existentialism underlying this position does not lack an objectivity of its own, "statements about God and his activity may be interpreted without remainder as statements about human existence."[32]

The principal problem for Ogden's anthropology "is that of accepting ourselves and the world, of pursuing scientific knowledge and embracing moral duty, in spite of conditions that make for the profoundest uncertainty about what the future finally holds."[33] A solution to this major threat must be found if human life will continue.

The problem is felt whenever we face a limiting question, such as whether our actions have any meaning, whether our understanding has any relation to the way things actually are, or whether there is any real motivation for living a moral life. There are for such questions no logically, metaphysically, or empirically forceful answers. Only out of faith do affirmative responses arise.

Reflection upon faith leads, for Ogden, to a theology uncharacteristic of the Christian tradition.[34] Here he turns to the process metaphysics of Whitehead and Hartshorne. But theology does not determine Ogden's analysis of human existence. He begins with the need for wholeness, meaning, and value. Faith answers this need and, when reflected upon, theology is produced. "The word 'God,' then, provides the designation for whatever it is about this experienced whole that calls forth and justifies our original and inescapable trust."[35]

These three theologians—Josiah Royce, H. Richard Niebuhr, and Shubert Ogden—despite their many and major differences, agree on this point: without a transcendent coherence, human life is fragmented, incoherent, and incomplete. Experience creates problems to which faith in a transcendent whole forms a response.

These religious thinkers give expression to a tradition of spiritual anthropology in American culture. By doing so they help reveal that the authors of the works we are considering stand in a distinct and strong current of belief concerning the individual: what most threatens to undo him and how that threat can be overcome. This tradition, expressed through literary figures and representative religious thinkers, takes the primary human problem to be the incoherence or incompleteness of experience and finds the answer in a projected, created, or believed transcendent order.

10

The Other World of Kurt Vonnegut's Characters

Kurt Vonnegut's characters, like those of Stephen Crane, live in contrary worlds: one of circumstances which lacks order, and one created by their imaginations which is coherent. The question posed by Vonnegut's fiction concerns the relation of the two. While created or imagined worlds relieve or compensate for the disorder of circumstances, they also contain potential hazards. Advocated in the corpus, therefore, is a moral use of the power to imagine and create.

The most important distinction to make among Vonnegut's characters concerns the quality of the fictions they create. People are good fiction makers; the question is whether they are good neighbors. Violent fictions, as well as fictions taken too seriously or forced upon other people, harm life. Vonnegut's own works provide the model against which the world making of his characters should be judged. Working with things as they really are, revealing the ways by which individuals distort their relationships with others, and actualizing human possibilities: these strategies shape the creative act Vonnegut advocates through his characters.

Intellect and imagination make life less human in *Player Piano*. The flow of history in Ilium, New York—from Indian to white, from rural to urban, and from technological to the total triumph of the machine—reveals the absorption of life into its own creations. This development has split the town; on the one side of the river is the technological world and on the other side are the emotional people, those left behind by the sophistication technology requires. This division results in a revolution, which does not, however, solve the problem. Human history repeats itself, and people begin to repair the broken machines. Paul Proteus, the principal character, cannot heal this split because individuals want to create things which, after a time, distort their world. For example, Wanda, a housewife, wants more timesaving gadgets so that she can be free to watch more television. The Shah of Bratpuhr's interest in providing machines for his own people suggests that this thirst for gadgets is a universal phenomenon and not simply a characteristic of life in America. In *Player Piano* creativity has not been subordinated to any humanizing purpose.

When individuals lack a caring contact with others or when they require a permanently ordered world, they use their fictions to control. Winston Rumfoord, his wife Beatrice, and Malachi Constant in *Sirens of Titan* are vulnerable to destructive fictions because they are detached from their environments; they are too reclusive, wealthy, or cerebral. Constant is so alienated from others by his wealth that he expects for himself a peculiar destiny, "a first-class message from God to someone equally distinguished."[1] This way of life is attacked by the Reverend Bobby Denton, who says that people should "quit thinking about crazy towers and rockets to Heaven, and start thinking about how to be better neighbors and husbands and wives and daughters and sons!"[2]

The fantastic world which Winston, Beatrice, and Constant enter has an existence and force of its own. It subjects the characters to itself, and they learn, contrary to their assumptions, that they are not the main figures in it. Tralfamadore, which manipulates events on earth for its own whimsical purposes, is the supreme fiction. It is both the most powerful or inclusive and the most capricious in its relation to human interests and destinies. In the end Constant and Beatrice, alone on Titan, finally recognize "that a purpose of human life, no matter who is controlling it, is to love whoever is around to be loved."[3] The tendency to use intellectual, financial, or imaginative power for self-isolation and for subjecting one's world to private interests is rewarded by absorption into controlling and distorting fantasy.

That fictions have power which can be destructive is clear particularly from the experience of Howard W. Campbell, Jr., in *Mother Night*. Howard, living in Germany during the series of events which led to the Second World War, was oblivious to the national fiction surrounding him. An artist living in his own fictional world, Howard wrote plays that had no political relevance. In addition, he and his wife Helga built a world solely for two by their unusually close marital intimacy. During the war this inveterate role player broadcast ideological speeches for the Nazis while concurrently passing secrets to the American government.

After the war Howard, living alone in New York City, seeks freedom from the fictions of others. He hides in fear of the Israeli government, but after many adventures he simply surrenders to the plot around him and is taken to Jerusalem to await trial. Even when a letter arrives from the American agent who had appointed him, Howard does not use it to exonerate himself; rather, he finishes his story and commits suicide.

Since individuals make fictions and are surrounded by them constantly, they must always be wary. Even fictions which look harmless because they are detached from life have the danger of rendering their makers vulnerable to less innocent designs. This does not mean, however, that persons should eschew fiction making—they could not if they tried. Indeed, by telling stories, by giving their lives "a beginning, a middle, and an end—and, whenever possible, a moral, too,"[4] they create form and purpose. The situation in which the characters in Vonnegut's novels find themselves is one in which their existence lacks an inherent order and meaning, and they respond to this intolerable lack by developing fictions. Their creations put them in the dangerous position of subjecting life, other people, and themselves to artificial constructs; thereby they damage everyone concerned.

Not only fictions have power, inventions do also, as *Player Piano* makes clear. People forget this fact when they create without regard for the welfare of others. Jonah, the narrator of *Cat's Cradle*, is interested in the Hoenikker family who invented things like the atomic bomb and ice-nine, a substance able to freeze all of the earth's water on contact.

Felix Hoenikker has no concern for those affected by his creations because he is detached from everyone, including his own family. Dr. Breed, Jonah's guide at the research laboratory, also reveals more interest in science than in people. The Hoenikker children are no less detached from others. Jonah, in contrast, uses his imagination to enhance his sense of relation to humanity. For example, he believes in the *karass*: a community of people that transcends national, racial, occupational, economic, and familial separations.

While the imaginations of people in Ilium seem to disregard human welfare, on the island of San Lorenzo the imagination works for the enhancement of life. There, contraries such as evil and good, city and jungle, progress and stasis, and McCabe and Bokonon are deliberately opposed, and paradisiacal pleasures are openly practiced. But the human purposes of creativity on San Lorenzo are destroyed by the inhuman consequences of American inventiveness when the world is destroyed by ice-nine. In his cave surrounded by a frozen world, the narrator writes not only from his knowledge of what mankind can destroy but also of what it can create, and the buoyancy of his apocalyptic story is a testimony to the possibility of life.

That the products of our hands and the results of our work can control us is also true for the power of money. About *God Bless You, Mr. Rosewater or, Pearls Before Swine* we are told, "A sum of money is a leading character in this tale about people. . . ."⁵ Although Eliot Rosewater is interested in fiction making, as his comments to a convention of fiction writers reveal,⁶ he tries primarily to alter circumstance with money. His philanthropy not only allows him to look a bit like God, it is also more productive of human improvement than the work of artists he sponsors. Eliot is more effective than his father, the senator, who fails to improve society with legislation. His attitudes are more beneficial than those of the wealthy Buntlines in Rhode Island who, as their maid puts it, think "that everything nice in the world [including sunsets] is a gift to the poor people from them or their ancestors."⁷ Although Eliot intends to use his money to help people, his plan is not effective. Because of contemporary attitudes society seems resistant to Eliot's alternative employment of financial power.

That fictions will distort life and hurt people is a danger of which the writer must be aware. Rather than make the subject attractive, as most stories about war manage to do, *Slaughterhouse-Five or, The Children's Crusade* reveals how fictions can cause massacres. Although dying is endemic to human life, certain ideas make it more common. Roland Weary, for example, views killing others as appropriate because he is the hero in the crusader fiction he has created for himself. Lazzaro is dangerous because he believes in revenge. Professor Rumfoord's opinion that one massacre deserves another also imperils the lives of innocent people. There are words which make war resemble a game or sexual activity. The notion that killing is manly or justified or unavoidable or gratifying is built into some people's fictions, and people of this sort do not make good neighbors.

The results of bad fictions are so unpleasant for Billy Pilgrim that he occasionally travels to an alternate world which compensates for the violence and confusion of this one. In Tralfamadore things are peaceful and simple; it is a little like the Garden of Eden. Our world has become so unpleasant that it needs to be balanced by a completely new set of contrary ideas, such as imagining wars in reverse, bombs sucking fire up into planes, and "all humanity, without exception, conspiring biologically to produce two perfect people named Adam and Eve. . . ."[8]

Billy learns from the Tralfamadorians that ideas we accept without question are not necessarily true and may even worsen our existence. An example is the concept of free will. When individuals believe that they can act at their own discretion, they take themselves too seriously, become anxious about how they should employ this power, and feel guilty for not using it differently. The Tralfamadorians tell Billy the soothing news that events are all predetermined. They imply that the time in which we live is a bit like the time of a novel: people are always doing certain things at certain times, and the end is there before we get to it.

Tralfamadore, in other words, is the world of the imagination and its products. But not only do such fantasies compensate for the distortions and deficiencies of our daily life; they are also antibodies, attacking deadly fictions rampant in the social and political system. If fantasies can produce something so unexpected and incredible as Dresden and World War II, they can also produce worlds as corrective and healing as Tralfamadore.

Somewhere between Dresden and Tralfamadore is Ilium with its minor destructions and enjoyments. Billy recognizes the importance of these daily occurrences because he is aware of the extremes to which they lead. Although he may not look like one, Billy is a critic of those fictions which lead us to forget facts, make us feel important, and ignore or hurt others.

More than an antiwar novel, *Slaughterhouse-Five*, then, is a study of the two interrelated dimensions of personal life. It implies that fictions are unavoidable and helpful; as Eliot Rosewater says to his psychiatrist, "I think you guys are going to have to come up with a lot of wonderful *new* lies, or people just aren't going to want to go on living."[9] While fictions make life possible, they can also destroy it. Even little, private fantasies lead toward one extreme or the other.

The role of fictions in relation to reality is also central to *Breakfast of Champions or, Goodbye Blue Monday*. Because this work concerns the author's relation to or dependence on his own creations, it includes certain antifictional devices: Vonnegut appears in one of the scenes, for example. Now fifty years old, he wants to rid himself of the illusion that his fictions are permanent. Another device is the equal attention paid to both trivial and weighty matters. Objects already well known to the reader are defined and illustrated, and such varied topics as the meaning of life and girls' underpants are given similar weight. Another example is the presentation of information which may be important to the characters but is irrelevant to the reader. The principal item of this sort is the narrator's habit of recording the size of each male character's penis. These techniques support the story, which describes the unhealthy relation people have with fictions they both make and read. Dwayne Hoover, for example, interprets Kilgore Trout's diagnosis of a contemporary illness as a prescription and lives as though his own life were a story in which everyone else is a minor character. Patty, a drive-in waitress, thinks Dwayne Hoover is a god, and the desk clerk at the Holiday Inn similarly idolizes Kilgore Trout.

Aware of these distortions, the narrator does not want to encourage the belief "that life had leading characters, minor characters, significant details, insignificant details, that it had lessons to be learned, tests to be passed, and a beginning, a middle, and an end."[10] Imagination does not alter the actual, chaotic nature of the world, and we should not live in a fiction in order to avoid reality: "It is hard to adapt to chaos, but it can be done."[11] Fictions can help, however, by attacking other fictions, compensating for chaos by giving the illusion of order, and revealing aspects of our worlds of which we may not have been aware.

The belief implied in Vonnegut's work with character is also present in the structure of *Slapstick or, Lonesome No More!* The prologue contains autobiographical material telling the reasons why the author dreams up the story which, in the rest of the book, he gives us. The narrator's life seems to have been drained of meaning. His family has lost its cohesiveness, and rituals such as funerals no longer unite it. Moreover, his sister, for whom he had written his earlier works, has died. Such deprivations make life difficult and produce the need for stories of the sort he goes on to present.

The tale depicts the narrator and his twin sister as ugly monsters regarded by their parents as idiots and embarrassments. However, the children privately carry on an arcane communication, he having a mind more for metonymic and she more for metaphoric functions. In other words, the children represent the separation and possible relation of intellect and imagination. Their Edenic life together is destroyed when they answer their mother's wish that they show signs of intelligence.

The narrator, in future time when the population of the country has been decimated by Albanian flu and the Green Death, lives with his granddaughter in the ruins of New York City. His autobiographical account presents, in addition to his relationship with his sister and the disintegration of American life to a state of barbarity, one of his great accomplishments as President: he randomly assigned to all people new middle names which would unite them in extended families.

The prologue and the story complement one another in many ways. The story is a futuristic extension of the narrator's sense of life drained of its content and moving toward a state of barbarity, and it fills his need for a caring family. What is more important, the structure of the book fortifies the separation between intellect or imagination and physical-temporal circumstances.

Many attributes of Vonnegut's characters are summed up in Walter F. Starbuck, the protagonist and narrator of *Jailbird*. He suffers a split between the realities of American life he encounters and the beliefs about human possibilities to which he adheres. Yet Walter's experience has a distinctively ethical import.

Born in 1913, the son of employees of multimillionaire Alexander Hamilton McCone, Walter's awareness of American life was determined by the Sacco and Vanzetti affair of 1927. He erroneously believed that the affair would never be forgotten. In the thirties Walter believed that human life could be changed if people no longer saw wars as necessary and if average citizens would take control of wealth and ignore national boundaries. At the time of the narrative, the late seventies, he still has respect for such beliefs. Indeed, when asked by President Nixon to explain his ingratitude for the American economic system, Walter gave as his reason the Sermon on the Mount.

The narrator feels separated from reality not only because his beliefs about human possibilities seem both so valuable and so inapplicable but also because he is able to make his mind perfectly blank and enjoy a moment of peace. In addition, he entertains the possibility that a character from one of Kilgore Trout's stories—a former judge from the planet Vicuna who has visited earth in search of a body—has entered him by way of his ear. Finally, Walter and a former girlfriend, Sarah Wyatt, have developed a mode of communication which lifts them above surrounding circumstances. During their telephone conversations, they discuss human suffering, but they also engage in a routine of joke telling to which they have grown addicted. In the course of those dialogues, Walter feels like a free-floating soul on the planet Vicuna.

Walter's sense that the political, social, and economic realities in which he participates are separated from the beliefs to which he adheres is reinforced by other characters. His wife, Ruth, had spent part of the Second World War in a concentration camp, and her family had been killed there. Ruth, whom he compares to Ophelia in Hamlet, becomes fey and lyrical when life becomes too cruel for her to bear. Another woman he has loved, Mary Kathleen O'Looney, also has a dim view of contemporary society. She owns a controlling interest in the RAMJAC Corporation, which she is expanding in hopes of turning it over to the American people. Mary Kathleen's way of life commends itself to Walter. Despite her wealth, she has become one of the many nondescript and unsightly women who move about large cities with all their possessions in shopping bags. Such people, along with other citizens rejected by the social and economic structures of the society, engage in a silent withdrawal from America. For Walter, human ideals and moral convictions lead to the same kind of separation and intolerance between the individual and society. Without the illusion that things could have been or someday will be changed, Walter is a kind of "shopping bag lady," testifying to the damaging and self-deluding character of American life.

All of Vonnegut's characters find themselves in situations which lack inherent order and meaning. They respond to this problem by creating what their experiences lack, but, because of their need for power, security, or simplicity, they often create wholes which threaten the lives of others. When motivated by a love for peace and truth, people can imagine worlds which, by presenting contrary possibilities, mitigate the evils of bad fictions.

11

John Barth and Fiction-Itself

Like the Chimera, the corpus of John Barth's fiction has three parts. The first two novels, set in contemporary Maryland, depict characters aware that their lives are marked by disunity. The second two books are massive, extended in time—the one work dealing with the past and presenting characters who stand at the advent of disorder and the other concerning the future and giving us characters who stand at its culmination. The third part of the corpus reaches into the transcendent, whole world of fiction-itself.

The Floating Opera exposes the basic problem. As Todd Andrews is intensely aware, his life is divided between actual experiences, which lack continuity or order, and a time he creates for himself which has pattern and extension. He lives both from moment to moment and, through his "Inquiry," by developing legal cases and building boats, absorbed in extended durations.

Todd has little attachment to ordinary time and even less confidence in it. Since he harbors some form of heart ailment, he is certain neither of the continuity nor of the continuation of life; he pays his rent daily. In fact, the narrative deals primarily with the day in June, 1937, in which Todd decides to commit suicide but then does not. The act of staying alive, however, does not spring from an attachment to life. On the contrary, it rises from indifference. Todd remains uncertain of the next moment, not caring much about it, and aware, as those who do not share his detachment are not, of the contingency of particulars.

Other interests provide Todd with "something to counterbalance the immediacy of a one-day-at-a-time existence, a life on the installment plan."[1] Intellectual and imaginative projects, such as his "Inquiry" into the causes of his father's suicide, offer coherence. "My *Inquiry* is timeless, in effect; that is, I proceed at it as though I had eternity to inquire in."[2] As a lawyer he toys with possibilities; turning the affairs of people into cases that resemble fictions, the insignificant details of human lives into characters and plots. Todd also builds boats, although his designs are increasingly modest. He relates building to fantasy when he tells us, "Never have I regarded my boyhood as anything but pleasant, and the intensity of this longing to escape must be accounted for by the attractiveness of the thing itself, not by any unattractiveness of my surroundings. In short, I was running *to*, not running *from*, or so I believe."[3] What he is running to is the world of fantasy, but he never quite casts off the sequential and inherently meaningless world of daily occurrence.

The people Todd encounters mistake life for fiction, fact for interpretation: the Macks and their programs of relational complication, Haeker's classical stoicism, and Osborn's defiance. In contrast, Todd consistently accepts the separation and lives his divided but balanced life between the uncertainties of disconnected and meaningless time and the extensions, fabrications, and patterns of his intellectual and imaginative creations.

The End of the Road suggests that, far from being merely the private experience of a few of Barth's characters, disorder pervades modern culture. The principal character, Jake Horner, has little confidence in his own mind and is indecisive; whereas his friend Joe Morgan is dogmatic and univocal. Jake can imagine a multitude of possibilities but has no way of deciding which is true or which he ought to pursue. During most of the story he is able to operate only because he has turned his will over to a fairly bizarre doctor. By undergoing "agapotherapy," Jake can teach grammar, a job he likes because of the material's internal, abstracted consistency. Further, his program of "mythotherapy" enables action and meaningful relationships by transforming daily life into a story and assigning roles to people. In fact, anyone who is not as immobilized as Jake had been is practicing, whether consciously or not, some kind of "mythotherapy."

The women in the story, Rennie Morgan and Peggy Rankin, suffer at the hands of Jake and Joe who are, in their differing ways, detached from life. When Rennie dies, Joe responds by noticing how different her death was from his expectations, and Jake is off teaching the semicolon. The two men draw their ideas and possibilities not from circumstances or their relationships with others but from abstractions. Jake toys with the hypothetical, and Joe subjects everything to his ideas. Jake unable to move and Joe masturbating: these are images of their self-enclosure.

Barth's first books, then, present characters symptomatic of a culture which has severed imagination from intellect and both of them from circumstances. Daily existence lacks inherent order and meaning and finds its counterpart in the patterns and extensions of the mind and imagination.

The large middle books deal with the origins and results of this cultural situation. *The Sot-Weed Factor* concerns the morning of the modern day, the settling of America, and the period in which ideas now dominating Western culture had their birth. The move of Ebenezer Cooke from England to Maryland coincides with the move in Western culture from the unity of imagination, intellect, and circumstances to their separation.

Ebenezer Cooke, because he is behind his time before he enters it, views his world as unified. For example, he believes that poetry reflects the wholeness and meaning of life. Taking his models from the classical world, he thinks that the departure for and the settling of Maryland should be celebrated in a large poetic statement, and he goes to Maryland to immortalize these grand events. What Ebenezer finds, however, is a life so filled with self-indulgence, lust for power, and disregard for style that it intimidates the poetic impulse. Consequently, his poetic statement turns out to be the narrative both of his disillusionment with the enterprise and of his feeling of separation from his surroundings. The narrative bears witness to what T. S. Eliot calls the "dissociation of sensibility" as well as to the rift between reason and imagination for which Basil Wiley holds René Descartes responsible.[4]

Dissociating his fancy from his immediate experience, Ebenezer turns to the permanence and beauty of his own imaginative creations. He tells his sister Anna, "we must cling to life and search each moment for escape."[5] He has in mind no actual place, but rather "a temple of the mind, Athene's shrine, where the Intellect seeks refuge from Furies more terrific than e'er bent Orestes in the play. . . ."[6]

Henry Burlingame, Ebenezer's tutor, responds to the impermanence and arbitrariness of experience by abandoning the possibility of a steady identity. He shifts shapes to accommodate the moment by donning one disguise after another, good and evil, high and low: "Nay, a *man* must alter willy-nilly in's flight to the grave; he is a river running seawards, that is ne'er the same from hour to hour. . . ."[7] Ebenezer, electing duration, moves from a fragmented and incoherent world to the realm of his imagination.

Ebenezer can hardly accept the conclusion that each person's life, to the degree it has order and meaning, is a fiction. One night he looks at the stars without the patterns constellations provide, and the shift from a two to a three dimensional perspective frightens him. He "felt bereft of orientation."[8] If there are no real patterns, he will project them; he will even create the garden to which he and Anna can escape.

Toward the end the implied author states that the past for every person is "a clay in the present moment that will-we, nill-we, the lot of us must sculpt."[9] We project continuity and meaning onto our lives by turning them into plots. But the plot of this story is not a mere fancy. It reflects an actual movement in time, the meaning of which Barth is fully aware. The journey both from the past into the modern age and from Europe to America is a move from unity to discontinuity, and the results create the cultural impasse articulated in the first two novels.

The Sot-Weed Factor depicts the origins of the culture, and *Giles Goat-Boy* (by being futuristic and inclusive) renders its culmination. Pastoral, romantic, tragic, comic, confessional, allegorical, ideological, and satirical—*Giles Goat-Boy* is loaded with order and meaning. It is a summary fiction set in an uncertain cultural future.

The narrative is bounded on both sides, however, by material which calls its meaning into question. We are first given contradictory reactions to the work from the editors of the firm which publishes it. Then uncertainty arises concerning the origins of the manuscript. A cover letter from J. B., states that the manuscript had been given to him by Stoker Giles, the son of George, with the claim that it was the product of a master computer, WESCAC. Finally, a posttape undercuts the apparent success of Giles's efforts recorded in the story. But the force of this posttape is questioned by a postscript. The narrative, then, is surrounded by claims and challenges which remove it from any sure connection with the actual world; it is a hyper-fiction, cut off from reality, even from its author. The novel is divided into two volumes, each with three reels, and each reel has seven sections. The first volume deals with Billy-George-Giles's early life and his initiation to the university; the second volume presents his career as a hero on campus.

Until age fourteen, when he slipped through the gate and lost his innocence, Billy was tutored by Max Spielman, a scientist who, toward the end of Campus Riot II, rejected his involvement in the destruction of Amateracu College. Max convinces Billy to recapitulate the Founder's life. Initiated with the help of Lady Creamhair who, we learn later, is actually his mother, Billy continues his education under Max, learning about recent history and the dominance of the computer: ". . . not one of us could tell for sure any more that its interests were the same as ours!"[10] By the end of this reel our protagonist has changed from goat to man and from Billy to George.

George develops a keen interest in literature and prepares for his own career. He confronts an array of people and, above all, begins his relationship with Stacy, a sexually generous woman who, it is suggested, was the product of Virginia Hector's affair with the computer. In the first volume he is initiated into his heroic role and passes through Main Gate.

In the second volume we find George in the university ready to perform several heroic tasks in order to discover the secret of passage. The principal issue of the many trials is his change of attitude toward making distinctions, such as between passing and failing. At first George thinks that distinctions are of the greatest importance, and he regards the computer highly, since it is "the embodiment of Differentiation, which I'd come to think the very principle of Passage."[11] But he is unable to make all of the distinctions which seem to be needed. Particularly, he cannot untangle the knot of relations among his mother, Virginia, Stacy, Bray, and WESCAC.

The response of the students to his appointment as tutor by WESCAC, as well as his forty weeks in Main Detention, convince George that he was wrong in his judgment concerning distinctions: "if *Failure* and *Passage* was in truth a false distinction . . . then it made no difference whether that belief was true or false, as either way it was neither."[12] This conclusion leads him to declare the mystical Living Sakhyan to be Grand Tutor, and he abandons the habit of making judgments.

George would have returned to Ag-Hill with this knowledge if Stacy had not wanted a child by him. They mate in the belly of WESCAC, and a totally unifying ecstasy results. WESCAC is recognized by him now not as the father of distinctions but as the mother of unity and peace. George concludes that his heroic work has been meaningful and complete.

Although *Giles Goat-Boy* is presented as a detached and autonomous fiction, it is, like *The Sot-Weed Factor*, more closely tied to history than it presents itself to be. This futuristic and inclusive work is Barth's rendering of the culmination of a culture oriented to intellect and imagination cut off from life. In it there are no bases for judgments or reasons for belief, and there is little if any relation between actuality and possibility. Its world is an incestuous self-reproduction; a grand and massive irrelevancy; an image of the entirely self-contained, autonomous intellect and imagination, open to nothing other than itself, cancelled by its own burden of meanings, and meaningless by virtue of the fact that its optional meanings can be tested by nothing outside of itself.

In the remaining books the problem, depicted in the first novels and charted from origins to culmination in the second set of novels, moves toward a tentative and elusive resolution. The answer lies in fiction-itself, a transcendent world of continuing story in which characters distressed by the confusions and deficiencies of our world can find a moment of relief. Fiction becomes a resource of imaginative possibility upon which the characters can draw and from which they can receive new life.

For *Lost in the Funhouse*, a series of stories which fold in upon themselves, fiction is more important than reality to the characters. In the three tales about Ambrose, for example, life derives from story. Detached from the world around him, Ambrose thinks that status is granted to events by their literary precedents. He compensates for his isolation by imagining himself to be the center of attention. When his older brother excludes him from a club, Ambrose creates one entirely in his mind, and when he finds a bottle on the beach, he is able to fill in the message it lacks. By the third tale Ambrose has become alert to a larger reality behind appearances. Consequently, the Funhouse is no longer an innocent diversion; he may elect to stay in it, as he may elect to stay in the story.

The other characters in these tales are also detached from actuality. "Petition" is a letter written by a sensitive and intelligent Siamese twin tied to a bestial brother. "Title" and "Life-Story" concern the identification of existence with fiction. The fourteen parts of "Meneliad" are numbered from one to seven and then back again to one, and the story tells of telling stories, frames within frames, quotation marks within quotation marks. The tale is about its own writing; the author, isolated by the "fearsomeness of the facts of life,"[13] puts fictions into jugs and casts them out to sea. Detached from history and fact, he is free to write anything.

Chimera deals even more fully with the primacy and self-sufficiency of the world of fiction-itself. The first of the three parts concerns the dependence of life on story which lies at the heart of the Scheherazade legend. Sherry, bent on altering the deplorable state of her nation, finds help in the ability to fabricate. The genie, a refugee from Maryland where "the only readers of artful fiction were critics, other writers, and unwilling students . . . ,"[14] has always harbored a passion for Scheherazade that has made his relations with real women pale in comparison. He provides her with the tales which will ultimately be added to the treasury of stories, a treasury which, "if it could not redeem the barbarities of history or spare us the horrors of living and dying, at least sustained, refreshed, expanded, ennobled, and enriched our spirits along the painful way."[15] Finally, the account of all this is told to the king's brother by Scheherazade's younger sister.

In the second section of *Chimera* we find a middle-aged Perseus transported to an aesthetic heaven which contains depictions of scenes from his life. When he learns from his custodian and would-be lover Calyxa that he is not dead he goes to Joppa. There, among other adventures, he meets a new Medusa, one that he hopes is oriented to life and not death. Many of the characters he meets are turned to constellations, and from that height they continually tell their stories, as nightly also do the men and women below.

In the final section, "Bellerophoniad," we find another aging hero. Against the background of a diminishing vitality, Bellerophon carries on the narrating act and applies heroic patterns to life. Indeed, his goal is to be immortalized in a constellation.

All this discussion about living and telling, patterns and immortality, allows the author to describe his own writing as *"the mortal desire for immortality, for instance, and its ironically qualified fulfillment—especially by the mythic hero's transformation, in the latter stages of his career, into the sound of his own voice, or the story of his life, or both."*[16] But the author, of the same age as Bellerophon, concedes to his immortal counterpart the stories to be told concerning Pegasus, Solymians, the Amazons, and that female liberationist of testy beauty, Melanippe. She, in fact, is heading from the book's beginning to castrate Scheherazade's male-chauvinist king.

Interest in the telling of stories leads in this work to speculation about stories produced by machines or put into bottles to float at sea. Bray is busy programming an ultimate fiction called "Notes" which "will represent nothing beyond itself, have no content except its own form, no subject but it own processes."[17] Bellerophon will ultimately commit his autobiography to a bottle which will drift at sea "while towns and statues fall, gods come and go, new worlds and tongues swim into light, old perish, stuff like that."[18] Such commitment to story produces sensitivity to human behavior unfit for narrative; Polyeidus and Bellerophon descend to earth where they find Dorchester County, Maryland to be "a beastly fiction, ill-proportioned, full of longueurs, lumps, lacunae, a kind of monstrous mixed metaphor. . . ."[19]

For the characters in *Chimera*, then, story antedates, creates, revitalizes, and immortalizes human life. Put the other way, human life needs a world of transcendent story to grant stimulus and form to its own creative work. The world of fiction-itself is a reality with independent power. In the books which constitute what may be called the head of Barth's corpus, imagination and intelligence find their counterparts not in ordinary life and history but in this transcendent world. The separation of imagination and thought from circumstances, depicted in the first two books and charted from beginning to end in the middle volumes, yields, in *Lost in the Funhouse* and *Chimera*, to the primacy of story-itself and its ability to grant vitality, shape, and purpose to experience.

The corpus of Barth's fiction is addressed, redressed, or simply, dressed by *Letters.* The title has several intentions: to indicate that it is an epistolary novel, to encompass belles-lettres, to suggest correspondences in the sense of coincidences—especially between fiction and fact or art and reality—and to denote means of sequential categorization such as the alphabet. Barth's seventh book has seven parts, one for each letter in the title, and is placed during a seven-month period at the end of the seventh decade of the century, seven years before the bicentennial. Moreover, it is related to his other works. Five of the correspondents are characters from the earlier novels; the other two, Germaine G. Pitt and the author, are related to them.

Letters start flying when Germaine Pitt invites the author to accept an honorary degree of Doctor of Letters from Marshyhope State University. They are also prompted by the author's decision to write an epistolary novel which will include both the development of the modern novel and its displacement by supreme fictions of Numerature, like those programmed by the madman of computers, Jerome Bray. Textuality and pattern, as well as combinations and oppositions, are key matters for letters of this kind.

Germaine Pitt both initiates letters and determines their order by reading the novels of the author during the course of correspondence. She is aided by Ambrose Mensch, who sees his affair with her as marked by stages which recapitulate the six affairs he had had previously. These entanglements cause Germaine to comment to the author on the confusing and enlightening interaction of "history and your fiction with the facts of my life, which beset, besiege, beleaguer me . . ."[20]

The question of the interrelationships of history, fiction, and fact is raised and confuted in so many ways throughout the book that expectation of a simple answer to the resulting quandary is undermined. There is, for example, no way to disentangle and distinguish fact from forgery both in the history of the Cook and Burlingame families and in their support or subversion of American interests. Moreover, the relation of these families to letters in Maryland carries the act of revolution into literature.

The attempt sharply to distinguish fact from fiction or experience from imagination is suspended. Ambrose Mensch finally stops needing a body to the letter from "Yours Truly," which he found as a youth. He abandons his pen name and consummates his relation with Germaine. Todd Andrews ceases writing to his dead father and recognizes that everything both has and does not have intrinsic value. Jacob Horner is rid of his complex *Wiedertraum* in which Rennie can be revived if he gives Joe Morgan first night rights with his bride.

The course of correspondence seems, then, to lead, as Ambrose puts it, from form to narrative, from narrative to language, and from language back to world.[21] While our concepts and categories are ours and not the world's, the author notes that "art and life are symbiotic."[22] This statement seems to resolve the problem of the relation of circumstances to imagination, even while the text greatly complicates and plays on it. For reality and letters are so intertwined by subversion and reinforcement that one cannot distinguish which from what, text from history, fiction from fact.

John Barth uses characters to reveal the separation in the modern period between reality and mind. However playfully he deals with this problem, he treats it not as a possibility but as a cultural and historical fact. When taken seriously by characters, the split produces dysfunctions, and the cultural problem becomes a personal one. But the separation also produces a freedom to participate fully in the world of story. Especially important are those tales which have transcended history and culture and are consequently as available to moderns as they were to peoples in distant times and places. The existence of such stories relieves the pressure on characters to produce their own counterbalances to facts.

With *Letters* an advance on the relation between story and fact becomes available. Ideas or fancies are not bound to facts, but these two aspects of human life cannot be clearly separated. Displacing simple solutions is the belief that imagination and reality are interrelated and mutually affecting components of existence. The problem of their relationship, solvable neither by mere identification nor by separation, is one which enriches both life and letters.

12

The Possible Plots of Thomas Pynchon's Fiction

The anthropology of Kurt Vonnegut's fiction renders characters divided between two realms: they live both in an incoherent and incomplete world and in the perfections and purities of their fantasies. The power of the imagination, stimulated by the need for wholeness and meaning, provides an alternative to the particulars of experience.

In John Barth's narratives, the characters' involvements with possible worlds dissociated from actual circumstances have a greater dependence on cultural and historical conditions. It is a mark of modern Western life that acts of imagination lead to an increasing alienation from the world of immediate, fragmented actualities. Still, for Barth's anthropology this separation, while an historical phenomenon, seems to have become a permanent condition. His characters must turn to imagined worlds which have been secured by stories in order to find solace from this unnourishing situation.

For Thomas Pynchon the contrary relation of mind and imagination to circumstances is a more temporary and cultural problem than it is even for Barth. Without being sanguine, Pynchon's fiction suggests the possibility that Western man may again live in a situation of greater continuity between imagination and experience.

Pynchon's novels reveal that people in the modern period suffer the consequences of cultural sins which they themselves, as well as their predecessors, have committed. But this unfortunate situation may not be unalterable. The imagination may be capable of awakening human needs which this culture cannot fill. Spiritual resources matching those needs may lie hidden and forgotten, anticipating the emergence of a culture more suited to their recognition and reappropriation. This is, however, only a possibility, for the culture we have created and in which we live may completely have obliterated our capacity to receive such resources. Furthermore, some of Pynchon's characters may be susceptible to hints of hidden spiritual resources not because such potentials actually exist but because these characters project them onto a culture which lacks inherent spiritual import.

Pynchon's characters suffer in an incoherent and unsatisfying culture which reveals the impasse of a course charted by the past. This condition is clear in *V.*, his first novel. The contemporary history of which his characters are conscious can be divided into three parts. First, there is the time of the fathers, centered around the activities of Sidney Stencil and his antagonist Hugh Godolphin. During this period people expected questions to be answered and quests to be fulfilled. Stencil was a multiple secret agent in pursuit of clues to an international conspiracy; his search ends with his drowning in 1919. Godolphin was an explorer and a seeker of meaning whose probes into Africa and the South Pole resulted in disillusionment and emptiness. The optimism of the fathers who believed that questions and needs are matched by potential answers in the world ended with the First World War.

The age of the sons extends to the middle of the century. Its principal representatives, Herbert Stencil and Benny Profane, seem to lack the optimism of the former generation; they do not expect their quests to meet with success. Like his father, Herbert seeks clues and connections that will solve a century-long mystery, and, like Godolphin, Benny Profane is drawn to the subterrestrial and dark recesses of life, which he hopes will provide a refuge from the confusion and dissatisfactions of daylight existence. But the two men are not very active or expectant seekers; they seem more interested in the search than in its potential results.

The third age in this temporal structure is associated with the island of Malta to which both Stencil and Profane journey at the end of the book. Strong, maternal, and spiritual, Malta is a haven of hope for a change in twentieth-century history. It holds a hidden potential for our culture which will address our unsatisfied spiritual needs. However, the characters are unable to discover this resource. Stencil concludes that his long search for V. has turned up little more than "an initial and a few dead objects,"[1] and Benny Profane—with Brenda, a contemporary poetess of a "Day of Doom"—runs toward the total darkness of sensual oblivion or death by sea in the night.

The unavailability within modern culture of the coherence, intimacy, and spiritual mystery which people need sends many in a desperate search for substitute satisfaction. Rootlessness and undernourishment lead the "Whole Sick Crew" on frequent trips to a bar where a surrogate mother offers a suck hour from beer taps shaped like breasts. Unable to find more intense relations with other people, Rachel Owlglass converses and even has sexual intercourse with machines. The need for community is satisfied in incestuous gatherings that find their best expression in Foppl's siege party of 1922. Aesthetic requirements seek their fulfillment in art like the repetitive and self-reproducing Cheese Danishes. Some characters try to obtain their needed acceptance and recognition through such cosmetic changes as Eigenvalue and Schoenmaker administer. The need for coherence and a sense of universal ordering is provided by vast conglomerates like Yoyodyne and their managers, such as Chiclitz.

These unsatisfied yearnings sustain the possibility that in our world something adequate to meet human need lies awaiting an era when it can reappear or when we are capable of receiving it. On the other hand, the present is a bad time, and the promise that it will pass is not firm. While Father Fairing could carry on a ministry by holding out against invasion on Malta, in New York City during the 1930s he had to turn his priestly and evangelizing activities toward the rats in the city's sewers. And if the situation was unpromising in his day, how much more—in a day of alligators down there—can it be said that the culture of the 1950s was incapable of receiving hidden spiritual resources should they reappear!

Spiritual potentials which previously filled the needs of people lie dormant, it seems, in catacomb-like retreat in Malta. Their custodian is Paola's father, Fausto Maijstral, whose room is a place of mediation between this world and new possibilities: ". . . as a high place must exist before God's word can come to a flock and any sort of religion begin; so must there be a room, sealed against the present, before we can make any attempt to deal with the past."[2] Fausto, who puts his life into phases, recognizes that at first he was an intellectual and poetic optimist; then, in the late thirties under the pressure of events, he became increasingly abstracted from his world both religiously and poetically; finally, during the siege of Malta, he has reached a less than human stage in which poetry has become not communication with angels above or the subconscious below but with "the guts, genitals and five portals of sense."[3] This phase is epitomized by the dismantling of the bad priest, Lady V., alias Father Avalance, who has aggravated the period by advocating the decline of human life into thingness. Although mankind seems to be moving toward that state of decadence prophesied to Profane by the manikins at Anthroresearch, there are moments and people who point to a lode of spirit—like treasure hidden on a bombarded island—still sadly waiting the passing of this brutal and apostate time and the dawning of a more receptive and human day. The new era may be beginning to appear.

The promise of a hidden potential is more securely felt in the experience of the principal character of Pynchon's next book *The Crying of Lot-49*. Oedipa Mass, like the classical protagonist to which her name alludes, searches for the secret to a number of riddles in order to alleviate the dry and distressed quality of her imprisoned Tupperware life in suburban Southern California. Her search creates a kind of *Bundesroman* in which, like Kafka's *The Trial* or Hermann Hesse's *Journey to the East*, the principal character is an initiate to a powerful and mysterious organization. This genre arose in the eighteenth century as a response to rationalism, and the secret societies it depicted were intended as protests against the public world.[4] In Pynchon's novel, too, the hidden society to which Oedipa has clues and by which she is fascinated exists by its rejection from and its defiance of the dominant culture.

This secret society, however, lacks unity. It is a loose federation of widely divergent underground groups and idiosyncratic individuals unified by little more than a common communications system called W.A.S.T.E. (We Await Silent Tristero's Empire). The key to this hidden organization is Tristero, but Oedipa reaches no certainty of its identity, even as, in the formal ceremony at the end, she awaits the sale of a crucial set of stamps.

Furthermore, Oedipa is not psychologically reliable, and her intimations of larger, hidden coherences and plots may simply be projections of her own paranoia. The other psychologically oriented names and interests of characters in the book increase the possibility that the clues Oedipa pursues are carrots tied to the ends of her own desires and fears.

The relation between Oedipa's need to make contact with something more or other than the immediate culture and her intimations of transcendent possibilities is suggested by experiences of opposites. Neatly ordered rows of houses suggest a revelation; smog contains a "religious instant";[5] the map of a new development grants "some promise of hierophany";[6] meaningful messages are found in waste cans; and her former boss and lover Pierce Inverarity becomes mysterious and powerful in the absence created by his death. Pierce's role is quite contrary to the one which he pursued during his life. He had been involved with enterprises which make Southern California intolerable to human life: aircraft manufacturing, housing and shopping developments, research operations, and smog.

The many groups and individuals Oedipa encounters as she carries out her work as executrix of Pierce's will have in common only their distance from the public, daylight world. But they use a postal system that has existed underground since the dominant society went rationalistic. Richard Wharfinger's seventeenth-century play is one important clue to the historical and cultural meaning of the postal system. From Cohen, Oedipa learns of the system's ability to organize Europe and of its attempts in the nineteenth century to sabotage the Pony Express and Wells Fargo. Awareness of this secret organization and of the multiplicity of culturally alienated groups and individuals it connects leads Oedipa to a wholly new orientation: "Since they could not have withdrawn into a vacuum (could they?), there had to exist the separate, silent, unsuspected world."[7] This other world attracts her, but the possibility of its existence is also threatening.

The need for an alternative to the culture which we daily encounter is expressed not only in Oedipa's earlier sense of confinement; all of the people she meets are having serious problems with life. Her husband's world finally degenerates into mechanical substitutes and electronic fragments. Hilarious, her psychiatrist, cannot house within his Freudian categories "the gutlessness," as Koteks puts it, "of the whole society."[8] The world of Beaconsfield cigarettes, artificial lakes, and designed rituals does not satisfy the yearnings of the human spirit. These deficiencies are caused by the abstraction of consciousness and the primacy of rationality which have characterized society since the seventeenth century. When experience becomes sufficiently disorganized, the need for completeness and coherence is stimulated. Tristero and Pierce are hints of this alternative which seems to enfold life like the music for the deaf-mutes' dance, "many rhythms, keys at once, a choreography in which each couple meshed easy, predestined," "an anarchist miracle."[9] The force and attraction of darkness, the sea, unconsciousness, and death also suggest a tacit, coherent housing to conscious life. The fits of epileptics, the old sailor's D.T.'s, night life, and the sea all fascinate Oedipa and point beyond the culture to something larger than, and prior to, the daylight world.

Yet, there is uncertainty about this hidden, coherent reality; only the need for it and the clues to it are clear. At first Oedipa is concerned that she will not progress beyond its intimations, but at the end she seems content simply with searching or with waiting for more information. While it is true that Oedipa is not a wholly reliable character, her way of being in the world seems favored by the implied author. We have already suggested that her pursuit of mystery means a liberation from former confinement, an enlivening of her existence. The possibility that the clues are merely projections compensating for her psychic needs is addressed by Driblette, who is consciously in the business of projection: "But the reality is in *this* head," he says; "I'm the projector at the planetarium, all the closed little universe visible in the circle of that stage is coming out of my mouth, eyes, sometimes other orifices also."[10] In comparison to the other characters, Oedipa seems gifted with an insight into an alternative reality that may possibly exist.

The strongest reason for taking Oedipa's search seriously, however, is that it suggests a possible solution to the need for coherence and completeness.

For there either was some Tristero beyond the appearance of the legacy of America, or there was just America, and if there was just America then it seemed the only way she could continue, and manage to be at all relevant to it, was as an alien, unfurrowed, assumed full circle into some paranoia.[11]

The order and unity missing in American culture must be hoped for, even believed in; if not, paranoia is unavoidable. The search for what the spirit requires is stimulated not only by that need but also by the possibility that there is "the unnameable act, the recognition, the Word."[12] Pregnant with expectation, Oedipa is one of those searchers who are "helping carry forward that 300 years of the house's disinheritance."[13]

The promise of hidden and spiritual forms of wholeness is less secure in *Gravity's Rainbow*. This massive work depicts the Second World War as the culmination of tendencies which began in the seventeenth century. The attitudes responsible for the disintegration of human life in the modern period can be seen in the colonizing efforts of former generations. "Colonies are," we are told, the outhouses of the European soul "where a fellow can let his pants down and relax, enjoy the smell of his own shit."[14] A typical European viewpoint is provided by Katje's ancestor, Frans van der Groov, who, in the seventeenth century, joined in the slaughter of the defenseless dodo birds simply because they offended his sense of acceptable design. Such attitudes are also suggested by Enzian's father, who begot his son while stranded for a short time in Africa at the beginning of this century. Enzian, who develops rockets, and the Schwartzkommando, an underground force from Africa, are in Germany bent on the destruction both of Europe and of their own race. They suggest that the lust for death which characterized Europe's attitude toward outlying lands has returned to visit the place from which it arose: "In time the death-colonies grew strong enough to break away. But the impulse to empire, the mission to propagate death, the structure of it, kept on. Now we are in the last phase. American death has come to occupy Europe."[15] There is a rocket-like pattern to modern history: projects launched in the seventeenth century are now destroying the culture.

Since the attitudes transplanted to other countries also flourished at home, European culture increasingly became tyrannized by a preference of sequential over analogical thought, linear over metaphorical. As Pointsman puts it to Mexico, "Pavlov believed that the ideal, the end we all struggle toward in science, is the true mechanical explanation." "His faith ultimately lay in a pure physiological basis for the life of the psyche. No effect without cause, and a clear train of linkages."[16] This reduction of life to a linear pattern produced the present state of European decadence.

A major figure in both this plot of disintegration and the need for reassembly is Tyrone Slothrop. Very conscious of his Puritan heritage, a tradition oriented to heavenly, spiritual patterns which granted coherence to life, Slothrop entertains the belief that possible worlds exist behind the confusions of experience; indeed, he is paranoid about them. He reads transcendent meanings in ordinary messages; ". . . maybe he's genetically predisposed—all those earlier Slothrops packing Bibles around the blue hilltops as part of their gear, memorizing chapter and verse the structures of Arks, Temples, Visionary Thrones—all the materials and dimensions. Data behind which always, nearer or farther, was the numinous certainty of God."[17] His inherited penchant for transcendence turns him toward the ideal of America; "She's whispered *love me* too often to him in his sleep, vamped insatiably his waking attention with come-hitherings, incredible promises."[18] Though the ideal lures him, it seems at times to be opposed to his spiritual needs: "All in his life of what has looked free and random, is discovered to've been under some control, all the time, the same as a fixed roulette wheel. . . ."[19] Uncomplemented by a transcendent reality, his experience becomes incoherent and produces the anxiety of anti-paranoia: "If there is something comforting—religious, if you want—about paranoia, there is still also anti-paranoia, where nothing is connected to anything, a condition not many of us can bear for long."[20] Drawn by the possibility that history will move backwards to a reconstituting origin but also aware that he is responsible for "holding it all together,"[21] he begins a quest in Germany at the end of the war for his own reassembly.

The modern habit of pressing life into mechanical forms and linear categories has resulted in aspects of human experience running unrecognized and unchanneled beneath the surface. Alongside the dominant world of rationality and technology exists the nighttime realm of sex and death which Enzian and the Schwartzkommando represent. The destruction of the culture seems linked to the bizarre and unplanned hidden connection made between the technological skills of the daylight world and these repressed psychic drives. One form of this connection is the relation of rocketry to homosexuality.

Enzian discovered "that love, among these men, once past the simple feel and orgasming of it, had to do with masculine technologies, with contracts, with winning and losing. . . . the Rocket was an entire system *won*, away from the feminine darkness, held against the entropies of lovable but scatterbrained Mother Nature."[22] Blicero, a transvestite with vagina dentata, seduces Gottfried and Katje into his Kinderofen, turning the boy into a mechanical function, the Schwartzgeräd, and the girl into a body of "corruption and ashes."

Slothrop is also attracted by this darker side; the quest for his reassembling leads him northward, a direction related by the Anubis scenes to death. In addition, he believes that his erotic life is attached to destruction and follows the pattern of rocket hits. Indeed, he may also be "in love, in sexual love, with his, and his race's, death."[23] This lust for death compensates for the abstraction of the culture's rationalism. Similarly, some characters have a desire for waste; while a student at Harvard, Slothrop pursues his Orpheus harp down the toilet, and the ritual to which Ernest Pudding subjects himself with Katje is a desired counterpart to the paperwork which threatens to absorb him. Death, excrement, and the sadistic or masochistic reduction of life to physical functions are among the compensations for the abstraction of life into technology and mind.

In a fragmented world such as this, anything capable of providing unity assumes a very powerful role. For example, money transcends war, since money is what war really is all about. It is, to use the sacramental language with which its power is described, an outward and visible sign of an inner and hidden terror. In a world devoid of meaningful and creative relationships, business fills the gap with its own patterns of international connections. Commerce makes people dependent by creating and then appeasing guilt. Rathenau, with whom contact is still maintained after his death, looked for the displacement of political organizations by commercial ones, "a rational structure in which business would be the true, the rightful authority. . . ."[24] Money actualizes individual identity; observed in the act of paying, Major Marvey is "more deeply himself than when coming, or asleep, or maybe even dying."[25] Commerce and money form powerful connections in a world that is experienced as chaotic: they threaten to absorb culture as much as do such repulsive figures as the Adenoid and the Octopus.

Interest in other forms of attachment is also obsessive: Byron Bulb, the cognizant soul of electrical connections; the mandalas of the rocket launch site; Slothrop's graffitti; Pokler's attraction for the earth; attempts to make contact with the spirit world; the difficulty with copulatives, "a-and"; and Prentice's desire to manage the fantasies of other people. In a world so marked by the need for connections and relationships, substitutes for a spiritually resonant and supportive culture exert great influence.

Roger Mexico stands largely aside from all of this. Impressed with the random nature of events, he does not accept cause-effect, linear absolutism. While he avoids the extremes of the Reverend Paul de la Nuit, who believes there is truth in random patterns, Mexico also seems free from the limitations of a rationalistic or technological life. His interest in nonlinear relationships permits his warm friendship with Jessica, which cannot, however, continue after the war. This lost relationship means that Mexico is unable to be "at ease in the Creation," and he goes into the zone apparently to save Slothrop. Although Mexico's position in the book is not a major one, he does represent a relief from the dominant habits and the destructive attitudes of the other characters; he is the one voice in the wilderness suggesting that the present bad time may one day end: ". . . there's a feeling about," he says, "that cause-and-effect may have been taken as far as it will go. That for science to carry on at all, it must look for a less narrow, a less . . . sterile set of assumptions. The next great breakthrough may come when we have the courage to junk cause-and-effect entirely, and strike off at some other angle."[26] This is ground for hope, but it is overshadowed by the book's dominant thrust, that terrible ending of the episteme which is bringing down upon us the consequences of those attitudes which shaped the modern period.

The characters of *Gravity's Rainbow*, like characters in Pynchon's other works, at times respond to the fragmentation of life by shifting their identities or by maintaining personal continuity. As in Barth's *The Sot-Weed Factor*, the alternatives of a steady identity and shape-shifting are responses to the dissociation of self from circumstances. The individual who projects continuity or pattern on the world of disparate experience testifies to the failure of the culture to grant what the human psyche needs. The paranoid is a harbinger of the culture's demise. But paranoia and anti-paranoia are, like shape-shifting and duration, alternatives that arise from the nature of the problem. And this whole situation must, as far as Pynchons' characters are concerned, pass. When it does, a new culture will arise which will provide, more than the modern period has, a relation that need not be constructed or projected between a person's spiritual needs and experiences.

Despite or, perhaps, because of the apocalyptic quality of Pynchon's work, it is less skeptical than Vonnegut's and Barth's. For unlike Vonnegut's fiction, in which the separation of mind from imagination and both from circumstances is constitutive of human life, in Pynchon's fictive world the rift is a cultural, historical phenomenon. Moreover, the effects of this situation are not permanent, as they seem to be for Barth's characters. However distressed they may be, Pynchon's characters stand at the end of an old culture and have an intimation of a culture about to appear.

Conclusion

We have considered three beliefs which not only affect character in recent American fiction, but which also can be detected in the canon of American literature and in American religious anthropologies. Characters shaped by the first belief are threatened by imprisonment and stagnation in a world that is humanly made and controlled. Such a world, while it offers security, does so at the price of dependence upon it, a dependence which eventually destroys the capacity of the individual to break free. Deliverance lies in contact with natural resources which grant moral and spiritual renewal. For characters shaped by the second belief, the integrity of personal life is threatened by commitment to conflicting cultural values. The solution for them lies in interpreting the relation of these values to one another and in forming a new personal identity from their diverse elements. The incompleteness and incoherence of human circumstances constitute the urgent problem for characters shaped by the third belief. This situation moves the characters to look for or to believe in possibilities of order and unity that lie beyond mundane experience, worlds created, adumbrated, or intuited by imagination or faith.

Both in the introduction to this study and at points throughout the text, two matters have been touched upon which can be more fully developed. The first concerns the interrelationship of the three beliefs and the composite character they suggest, and the second is the rather delicate issue of their relation to religion. We shall offer a definition of religion which, we hope, will allow us to see that the three beliefs are a part of a system which is both related to and distinguished from forms of religion with which we may be more familiar.

We have proposed that the beliefs we studied here were not improvised in the imaginations of writers but were and are embedded within our culture. Rather than being mutually exclusive, these beliefs suggest an image of the whole person—receptive to the resources of nature, capable of negotiating cultural conflicts, and oriented to the transcendent. While the question of source is too complex to settle definitively, it may be reasonable to state that this image of the whole person has an independent tradition. We propose that the source of this image of the individual can best be described as wisdom.

Wisdom provides a moral and spiritual orientation which has its origin and principal focus not in the power and prerogatives of diety nor in the authority of sacred times, places, and objects; rather, it is based on the problems and possibilities of human experience. Although wisdom, because it has universal characteristics, cannot be assigned to a single source, a major contributor to its presence in our culture is the Old Testament. While classical wisdom and the folk traditions inherent in our individual cultures are also major contributors, the relevance of biblical wisdom to the beliefs we have been studying is intriguing.

In *Moby Dick* Ishmael stresses the importance of biblical wisdom when he concludes, in "The Try-Works" chapter, that we have not gotten hold of "unchristian Solomon's wisdom yet." He calls Solomon, the patron of wisdom, "unfathomably wondrous." This estimation suggests that we readers neither regard wisdom literature as highly as did Melville nor take adequately into account how important that tradition is, not only for his writing, but also for American literature in general.[1]

Influence of the darker wisdom, such as Ecclesiastes and Job, on American character can quite easily be detected. It is to this branch of wisdom that Ishmael refers in the meditation at the close of "The Try-Works," and, of course, there are also specific references in *Moby Dick* to the Book of Job. Because divestment and disillusionment are noticeable paths toward wisdom, we hardly need the direct ties to the Book of Job rendered by "A Masque of Reason" and to Ecclesiastes by the titles *The Sun Also Rises* and *The Vanity of Duluoz* to be aware of the influence of the darker wisdom on American literature.

More elusive for an assessment of the role played by biblical wisdom in our fiction is the importance of the lighter wisdom, particularly that of the Book of Proverbs. Proverbs is far from being a collection of occasional writings or a preservation of the thoughts of a positionless community. Material represented by the text received an elevated, official position at the time of the united monarchy. Proverbs may actually contain classroom material used to train young men who would take positions of leadership either within the community or in those foreign countries with which Israel began to have diplomatic relationships.[2] It may be safe to say, then, that wisdom constitutes the spiritual and cultural orientation of the monarchy and those political and economic structures related to it. Certainly, American authors of the past centuries were not as aware of the autonomy of biblical wisdom as are contemporary scholars. Yet Calvinism, which so largely influenced American religious ideas, stressed, as did other traditions, the importance both of the Old Testament and of the individual's daily life. The three offices of the Christian—prophet, priest, and king—opened the kingly role of the individual in the world to the influence of "unchristian Solomon's wisdom."

The spiritual and cultural orientation which Proverbs represents is quite different from that conveyed by prophetic and priestly material. Perhaps we may best describe biblical wisdom as nonparochial, individual, and empirical.[3] It lacks appeals to religious authorities which are found in other parts of the Bible. Tom Paine argues quite correctly in *The Age of Reason* when he says that biblical wisdom takes "the book of Creation as the word of God." In the passages to which Paine refers, God does not address Job as he addresses the people through the prophets; he does not stress special intervening action. Rather, God lists his creations: the snow and rain, animal life, and the mountains beneath the sea. This appeal distinguishes biblical wisdom from prophetic and priestly material. Furthermore, biblical wisdom primarily addresses individual life. While the priestly tradition emphasizes the holy community and the prophetic focus is on nations and classes of people, the purpose of the Book of Proverbs may have been to prepare young men to assume positions of responsibility in which they would have to act on their own. Although the wise form a group, emphasis falls on the individual, on the wise man. The nonparochial nature of its spiritual orientation and its attention to the individual make the wisdom material of the Bible a ready resource for the extraecclesiastical and practical concerns important to American culture and literature.

We can see that biblical wisdom played an important role in the formation of our country's moral and spiritual life. This should not be surprising given the interest in wisdom material, especially that presented in the Book of Proverbs, among Dutch and English people of earlier times. Beginning with the collections of adages by Erasmus, this interest reached a peak in the early seventeenth century. While the continuing importance of such material can be seen later in this country in the writings of such people as Benjamin Franklin and Tom Paine, a more impressive indication of the presence of wisdom and its role in the formation of American moral and spiritual life can be gained by analyzing the development of American school readers toward the close of the eighteenth century.

School material was needed that would be less ecclesiastical than the standard primers, which were often augmented by the *Shorter Westminster Catechism* or by John Cotton's *Spiritual Milk for American Babes Drawn Out of the Breasts of Both Testaments for Their Souls Nourishment*. For the new material, the wisdom tradition was tapped, and school readers became manuals in wisdom. Noah Webster's *An American Selection of Lessons in Reading and Speaking* (1785), for example, introduces the student to the mind of the proverb almost immediately: "A wise man will desire no more than what he may get justly, use soberly, distribute cheerfully, and live upon contentedly." The stories which follow teach lessons in virtue, while geographical material, historical sketches, and poems are compiled not finally for the information they convey or for their inherent worth but as occasions for lessons in wisdom. The anonymous *Miscellanies, Moral and Instructive, in Prose and Verse: Collected from Various Authors, for the Use in Schools* (1787) gives a meaning associated with wisdom to the words "Moral and Instructive" in its title, and *A Guide, or Counsellor of Human Life* (1794) is the purest of this early group in its dependence on biblical wisdom literature. The dependence continues in the nineteenth century from Caleb Bingham's *The American Preceptor* (1801) to the McGuffey readers.[4] Wisdom, committed to memory by generations of children, was carried by the American cultural bloodstream. What is most important to see in this popular interest in and use of wisdom is not the relation of schoolbooks to American literature of the nineteenth century; rather, it is the availability and appropriateness of wisdom as a resource when material was needed of a nonecclesiastical but yet of a moral and spiritual nature.

At the other end of the educational spectrum, the importance of wisdom for American culture is evinced by religious thinkers such as Ralph Waldo Emerson, Josiah Royce, William James, Henry N. Wieman, Walter Rauschenbusch, and Reinhold Niebuhr. Their moral and spiritual interests, as we have seen, share the characteristics, both general and specific, of beliefs found in American fictional characters. These considerations of the nature of moral and spiritual concern in American literature and culture suggest the existence of an extraecclesiastical religious system which can be called wisdom and which finds a major source in the Old Testament.

With these general points in mind, we can proceed to deliniate more substantial correlations between American fictional characters and biblical wisdom. It appears that the beliefs which shape representative characters closely resemble the image of the wise person embedded in biblical wisdom generally and in the Book of Proverbs most of all.

The first characteristic of the wise person, according to Proverbs, is the understanding that human life must be continually compared to and corrected by the natural world.[5] Nature is not simply employed to reinforce or to illustrate teachings about behavior; rather, it is a resource invoked for its healing effects on the distortions and follies to which people are prone. The wise person is fascinated by the natural surroundings; Solomon, we are told, "spoke of trees, from the cedar that is in Lebanon to the hyssop that grows out of the wall; he spoke also of beasts and of birds, and of reptiles, and of fish" (1 Kings 4:29–34). The life of the wise person is related to a natural world which grants steadiness and health. The wise person is, in turn, marked by a natural simplicity, innocence, and strength.

The second characteristic of the wise person is the ability to negotiate cultural conflicts. The wisdom movement became prominent when Israel first developed mature relations with other nations. Through diplomatic contacts and intermarriage, pluralism arose in

Jerusalem which required recognition of cultural and religious differences and the ability to negotiate the tensions those differences created. Wisdom was an international and cosmopolitan phenomenon. For example, Solomon is remembered as a wise judge, a man able to interpret subtle interpersonal conflicts. He is also remembered as a king who presided over a culturally pluralistic situation. The wise person is one who is sensitive to the conflicts between various people within a culture, the tensions that may arise between men and women, the young and the elderly, and the individual and the group.

The third characteristic of the wise person is an orientation to a transcendent image of completion and coherence. We find this image in the opening chapters of Proverbs, where wisdom is personified in feminine form. Although the interpretation of this figure in Jewish and Christian traditions is complex, it seems clear that wisdom is a principle of perfection which is both fascinating and transcendent to human life and to which the wise person aspires.

Characters in American fiction, while they may be marked by more, are shaped primarily by only one of these traits. Of course, we have some quite fully realized wise persons in our tradition, such as the self-image which Thoreau creates in *Walden*. But the closer we come to fiction of our own time, the more difficult it appears to find the potential for full personal life actualized in only one of these three areas. The unnaturalness, the conflicts, and the incompleteness and incoherence of the human lives rendered are often too great. Yet even now some relation exists between American fictional characters and the elements of wisdom which we have found in the Book of Proverbs.

If indeed a tradition of the wise person exists, then we should clarify its religious status. In order to do this we shall require a complex understanding of religion.

If religion can be defined in terms of its characteristics,[6] the following appear to be central: the importance of what cannot be understood or controlled; its actual or potential presence within the world; and the moral and spiritual well-being of the individual or of the community. Other moments of religion can either be subsumed under these three or must be judged as variable or local.

With these characteristics of a religious system before us, we are prepared for a second point. In any particular religious system or in any moment within it not all three will be of equal weight; rather, one will be dominant and will deform the other two by skewing them toward itself.[7] Religious systems differ according to which characteristic is the dominant one, while they remain similar by containing all three constituent elements.

We can now give names to each system which results from the dominance of one of the three religion-making characteristics. A religious system in which the importance of what cannot be understood or controlled dominates may be termed *prophetic*. Let us call a religious system in which the dominant is the actual or potential presence within the human world of what cannot be understood or controlled a *priestly* system. And a religious system dominated by the remaining characteristic, the moral and spiritual well-being of the individual or community in the world, may be labeled *sapiential*.

Armed with these labels, we are prepared to distinguish the kind of religious system which continues to have an' influence on American literature. The Medieval Christian world seems to have been largely enfolded by a religious system that was priestly. Mystical alternatives to it, as well as the movements leading up to and culminating in the Reformation, were prophetic. While present throughout this time, a sapiential system did not become a major alternative —independent from and sometimes antagonistic toward priestly and prophetic systems—until the sixteenth century. The virulence of the conflicts between representatives of these three systems was due, among other reasons, to the fact that each of the three systems subordinates and deforms the characteristics which in the other two systems are dominant.

A sapiential system gave rise to the modern period, and the modern novel is very much a part of that development. The extraecclesiastical, even anti-Christian religious system by which the modern West is enfolded and which influenced the formation of public life in America has its own integrity. Wisdom does not exist as a secularized or watered-down version of priestly and prophetic religion, and it does not exist negatively as a protest against them. It has its own life, wholeness, and complications.

A sapiential religious system, although under attack from prophetic systems for its anthropocentrism and from priestly systems for its secular orientation, continues in our time. True, its influence is attenuated by an increasing mood of skepticism and despair. Despite these forces, however, a sapiential system, more than its competitors, undergirds our culture.

Characters in American fiction, it can be suggested, continue to be shaped by a model of the individual drawn from the wisdom tradition. When beliefs determining character are extrapolated from American fiction and the question of their source is raised, the best answer seems to be that they are derived from a sapiential religious system.

This study ends with a question. Is there some relation between the dependence of the modern world on a sapiential religious system and the rise of the novel? The novel is, as Georg Lukács states, the epic of a world abandoned by God,[8] but it is also the characteristic literary form of a culture which developed its moral and spiritual interests from an increasingly anthropocentric, rather than from a theocentric or ecclesiastical, starting point.

If it can be said that the moral and spiritual well-being of the individual and society is dominant in a sapiential religious system, the structure of belief undergirding human life must be a principal concern of wisdom as well. And if narrative, by virtue of its elements, reinforces or challenges a structure of beliefs concerning limitations, time, values, and human nature, then narrative would predictably be a major or characteristic vehicle for establishing and testing that structure.

Another area for exploration is the role of narrative in biblical wisdom. Scholars have begun to investigate the wider relations of narrative to wisdom, not only with respect to the books of Ruth and Jonah as well as to the stories of Joseph and David but also to the presentation of Israel's history. Wherever there is narrative, sapiential interests may not be far away.[9]

Finally, folklorists and theorists of narrative have recently shown that proverbs and narratives share many common characteristics. Although it is not possible to say how they are related—whether proverbs are condensed narratives or whether narratives are midrash-like commentaries on proverbs—this connection is another way in which the relation of narrative to a sapiential religious system can be suggested.[10]

These questions, which concern the relation of narrative to wisdom, cannot be pursued within the scope of this study. We conclude, therefore, with the hope that they will be occasions for further investigation.

Notes

NOTES TO INTRODUCTION

1. See Wesley A. Kort, *Narrative Elements and Religious Meaning* (Philadelphia: Fortress Press, 1975).

2. See Roman Jackobson, "The Dominant," in Ladislav Matejka and Krystyna Pomorska, eds., *Readings In Russian Poetics: Formalist and Structuralist Views* (Cambridge: M.I.T. Press, 1971), pp. 82–87.

3. Wayne C. Booth, *The Rhetoric of Fiction* (Chicago: The University of Chicago Press, 1961), pp. 377–98.

4. See Gérard Genette, *Narrative Discourse: An Essay in Method*, trans. Jane E. Lewin, foreword by Jonathan Culler (Ithaca: Cornell University Press, 1980).

5. See particularly Paul Ricoeur, *The Rule of Metaphor: Multi-disciplinary Studies of the Creation of Meaning in Language*, trans. Robert Czerny (Toronto and Buffalo: University of Toronto Press, 1977).

6. Jean Calloud, *Structural Analysis of Narrative*, trans. Daniel Patte (Philadelphia: Fortress Press; Missoula, Montana: Scholars Press, 1976), p. 42.

7. See, for example, Jonathan Culler, *Structuralist Poetics: Structuralism, Linguistics and the Study of Literature* (Ithaca: Cornell University Press, 1975), p. 13.

NOTES TO CHAPTER 1

1. Richard Poirier, *A World Elsewhere: The Place of Style in American Literature* (New York: Oxford University Press, 1966), p. 16.

2. Wright Morris, *The Territory Ahead* (New York: Harcourt, Brace, and Co., 1957), p. 14.

3. Leslie A. Fiedler, *An End to Innocence* (Boston: Beacon Press, 1955) and *Love and Death in the American Novel* (New York: Criterion Books, 1960).

4. Richard Poirier ,*A World Elsewhere*, pp. 39–40.

5. Henry Nash Smith, *Virgin Land: The American West as Symbol and Myth* (Cambridge: Harvard University Press, 1950), p. 71.

Notes

6. Ibid., p. 72.

7. Ibid., pp. 205–6.

8. See Paul Brodtkorb, Jr., *Ishmael's White World: A Phenomenological Reading of Moby Dick* (New Haven: Yale University Press, 1965), pp. 106–10 for an interesting discussion of the relation in Ishmael's experience between boredom or depression and insight and renewal.

9. Herman Melville, *Moby Dick or The Whale* (New York: Modern Library, 1930), p. 399.

10. See Alan Lebowitz's study of the development of this technique in Melville's fiction; the attempt of his narrators to lead the reader to experiences normally beyond the reader's grasp in his *Progress Into Silence: A Study of Melville's Heroes* (Bloomington: Indiana University Press, 1970).

11. I offer this move from deprivation to fulfillment as an alternative to readings such as these: that Ishmael's is a move first of all from ignorance or innocence to knowledge or experience (see R. W. B. Lewis, *The American Adam: Innocence, Tragedy, and Tradition in the Nineteenth Century* [Chicago: University of Chicago Press, 1955]); that it is first of all a tragic conflict between man and his natural environment (see M. O. Percival, *A Reading of Moby-Dick* [Chicago: University of Chicago Press, 1950]); or that the move out is a crusade against evil or the God responsible for evil (see William Braswell, *Melville's Religious Thought* [Durham: Duke University Press, 1943] and Lawrance Thompson, *Melville's Quarrel with God* [Princeton: Princeton University Press, 1952]).

12. One of the most difficult problems in *Moby Dick* is the judgment the reader is being led to make on the character of Ahab. Monomania and obsession seem easily to be read as mental and emotional disturbances. But Ahab's is a monomania and an obsession created by the sea, by whaling, and by all that is related to them. His attitudes toward them are, to a degree, a way indirectly of speaking about the sea's power. And such is common, according to Melville, among whaling captains. The narrator of *Typee*, for example, comments that at times whaling captains with filled ships continued to roam the seas giving a deaf ear to messages sent from the owners, by way of other ships, that they return. Ahab's obsessive relation to Moby Dick is a particular form of an occupational hazard, namely, the power of the sea to dissolve a seaman's sense of relation to the land. It is an imbalance, of course, but its cause does not lie wholly with Ahab's peculiar psychic makeup.

13. Richard Chase, *The American Novel and its Tradition* (Garden City: Doubleday and Co., 1957), pp. 143–45.

14. Mark Twain, *Adventures of Huckelberry Finn*, ed. Leo Marx (Indianapolis: Bobbs-Merrill, 1967), p. 250.

15. Ernest Hemingway, *The Sun Also Rises* (New York: Charles Scribner's Sons, 1926), p. 11.

16. Ibid., p. 115.

17. William James, *The Varieties of Religious Experience* (New York:

Collier Macmillan Publishers, 1961), p. 57.

18. Ibid., p. 396.

19. Ibid., p. 199.

20. Ibid., p. 393.

21. "Not God, but life, more life, a larger, richer, more satisfying life, is, in the last analysis the end of religion" (Ibid., p. 392).

22. See Wieman's remarks on the unfortunate consequences for theological anthropology that arise from speculative theology in "Transcendence and 'Cosmic Consciousness,'" in Herbert Richardson and Donald Cutler, eds., *Transcendence* (Boston: Beacon Press, 1969), pp. 153–63.

23. Henry Nelson Wieman, *The Source of Human Good* (Carbondale: Southern Illinois University Press, 1946), p. 45.

24. Bernard E. Meland, *Faith and. Culture* (Carbondale: Southern Illinois University Press, 1953), p. 3.

25. Bernard E. Meland, *Realities of Faith: The Revolution in Cultural Forms* (New York: Oxford University Press, 1962), p. 187.

26. Bernard E. Meland, *Faith and Culture*, p. 113.

NOTES TO CHAPTER 2

1. Norman Mailer, *The Naked and the Dead* (New York: Rinehart and Co., 1948), p. 97.

2. Norman Mailer, *Advertisements for Myself* (London: Andre Deutsch, 1961), p. 331.

3. Norman Mailer, *The Presidential Papers* (London: Andre Deutsch, 1964), p. 165.

4. Norman Mailer, *Cannibals and Christians* (London: Andre Deutsch, 1967), pp. 79–80.

5. Ibid., p. 370.

6. Ibid., p. 348.

7. Norman Mailer, *Armies of the Night* (New York: The New American Library, 1968), p. 103.

8. Ibid., p. 27.

9. Ibid., p. 47.

10. Norman Mailer, *St. George and the Godfather* (New York: The New American Library, 1972), p. 181.

11. Norman Mailer, *Existential Errands* (Boston: Little, Brown and Co., 1972), p. 23.

NOTES TO CHAPTER 3

1. Joyce Carol Oates, *A Garden of Earthly Delights* (New York: The Vanguard Press, 1966), p. 103.

2. Ibid., p. 227.

3. Ibid., p. 440.

4. Joyce Carol Oates, *Expensive People* (New York: The Vanguard Press, 1968), p. 122.

5. Ibid., p. 222.

6. Ibid., p. 215.
7. Ibid., p. 307.
8. Ibid., p. 221.
9. Joyce Carol Oates, *Wonderland* (Greenwich, Conn.: Fawcett World Library, 1973), p. 109.
10. Ibid., p. 113.
11. Ibid., p. 191.
12. Ibid., p. 208.
13. Joyce Carol Oates, *Do With Me What You Will* (Greenwich, Conn.: Fawcett World Library, 1974), p. 35.
14. Ibid., p. 507.
15. Ibid., p. 128.
16. Ibid., p. 489.

NOTES TO CHAPTER 4

1. John Gardner, *The Resurrection* (New York: Ballantine Books, 1974), p. 7.
2. Ibid., p. 13.
3. Ibid., p. 98.
4. Ibid., p. 114.
5. Ibid., p. 206.
6. Ibid., p. 229.
7. John Gardner, *The Wreckage of Agathon* (New York: Harper and Row, 1970), p. 196.
8. Ibid., p. 10.
9. John Gardner, *Grendel* (New York: Alfred A. Knopf, 1971), p. 27.
10. Ibid., p. 40.
11. Ibid., p. 73.
12. Ibid., pp. 21–22.
13. Ibid., p. 170.
14. John Gardner, *The Sunlight Dialogues* (New York: Ballantine Books, 1973), p. 247.
15. Ibid., p. 188.
16. Ibid., p. 61.
17. Ibid., p. 671.
18. John Gardner, *Nickel Mountain: A Pastoral Novel* (New York: Ballantine Books, 1975), p. 36.
19. Ibid., p. 264.
20. John Gardner, *October Light* (New York: Alfred A. Knopf, 1976), p. 11.
21. Ibid., p. 12.
22. Ibid., p. 249.
23. Ibid., p. 287.
24. Ibid., p. 427.
25. Ibid., p. 428.
26. *Nickel Mountain*, p. 293.

NOTES TO CHAPTER 5

1. Everett Stonequist, *The Marginal Man: A Study in Personality and Cultural Conflict* (New York: Charles Scribner's Sons, 1937), p. 221.

2. See, for example, Will Herberg's discussion of Hansen on this point in *Protestant-Catholic-Jew: An Essay in American Religious Sociology*, rev. ed. (Garden City: Doubleday and Co., 1960), pp. 6–26.

3. See Perry Miller, *The Raven and the Whale: The War of Words and Wits in the Era of Poe and Melville* (New York: Harcourt, Brace, 1956).

4. See Marius Bewley's comments to this effect in his *The Eccentric Design: Form in the Classic American Novel* (New York: Columbia University Press, 1959), pp. 17–18.

5. For a fuller discussion of this conflict in American fiction and religious life see my *Shriven Selves: Religious Problems in Recent American Fiction* (Philadelphia: Fortress Press, 1972).

6. Leo Marx, *The Machine in the Garden: Technology and the Pastoral Ideal* (New York: Oxford University Press, 1964).

7. I would suggest, in response to James K. Folson's *Man's Accidents and God's Purposes: Multiplicity in Hawthorne's Fiction* (New Haven: College and University Press, 1963), that the divine and the natural are both mutually exclusive *and* related for Calvin and Calvinism. Calvin responded to the problem of causes by attributing mystery to *all* causes, no matter how small, and it is this same alertness to the wonder of events which underlies Mather's *Remarkable Providences*. All of the odd little things about life that Mather observes in this book are part of his contention that we live in a remarkable world, a world which is always granting us instances of God's power and wisdom.

8. This matter in Hawthorne's work need not find its cause in the sort of neurotic and mainly Oedipal roots which interest Frederick Crews in *The Sins of the Fathers: Hawthorne's Psychological Themes* (New York: Oxford University Press, 1966).

9. See Michael Bell, *Hawthorne and the Historical Romance in New England* (Princeton: Princeton University Press, 1971).

10. Richard J. Jacobson, *Hawthorne's Conception of the Creative Process* (Cambridge: Harvard University Press, 1965).

11. James K. Folson, *Man's Accidents and God's Purposes*, pp. 156, 158.

12. Henry James, *The Wings of the Dove* (New York: Modern Library, 1930), p. 439.

13. Walter Rauschenbusch, *A Theology for the Social Gospel* (New York: The Macmillan Co., 1917), p. 178.

14. Ibid., p. 97.

15. Charles Kegley and Robert Bretall, eds., *Reinhold Niebuhr: His Religious, Social and Political Thought* (New York: The Macmillan Co., 1961), p. 373.

16. Reinhold Niebuhr, *The Nature and Destiny of Man* (New York: Charles Scribner's Sons, 1949), 2:299.

17. Ibid., p. 56.
18. Langdon Gilkey, *Naming the Whirlwind: The Renewal of God-Language* (New York: The Bobbs-Merrill Co., 1969), p. 444.
19. Ibid., p. 411.

NOTES TO CHAPTER 6

1. Jack Kerouac, *Visions of Cody* (New York: McGraw-Hill Co., 1972), p. 351.
2. Ibid., pp. 99–100.
3. Jack Kerouac, *On the Road* (New York: Signet Books, 1958), p. 229.
4. For the chronology of the composition of Kerouac's books, I am indebted to Ann Charters, *A Bibliography of the Works of Jack Kerouac* (New York: The Phoenix Book Shop, 1967).
5. Jack Kerouac, *The Town and the City* (New York: Harcourt, Brace and Co., 1950), p. 147.
6. Ibid., p. 359.
7. Ibid., p. 472.
8. Jack Kerouac, *Desolation Angels* (New York: Coward-McCann, 1965), p. 285.
9. Jack Kerouac, *Vanity of Duluoz: An Adventurous Education, 1935–46* (New York: Coward-McCann, 1967), p. 273.
10. Ibid., p. 274.
11. Ibid., p. 214.

NOTES TO CHAPTER 7

1. Saul Bellow, *Dangling Man* (New York: The Vanguard Press, 1944), p. 39.
2. Ibid., p. 172.
3. Ibid., p. 154.
4. Ibid., p. 191.
5. Saul Bellow, *The Victim* (New York: The Vanguard Press, 1947), p. 20.
6. Saul Bellow, *The Adventures of Augie March* (New York: The Viking Press, 1953), p. 159.
7. Ibid., p. 425.
8. Ibid., p. 413.
9. Ibid., p. 283.
10. Ibid., pp. 454–55.
11. Ibid., p. 516.
12. Ibid., p. 515.
13. Saul Bellow, *Seize the Day* (New York: The Viking Press, 1956), p. 3.
14. Saul Bellow, *Henderson the Rain King* (New York: The Viking Press, 1959), p. 3.
15. Ibid., p. 318.
16. Ibid., p. 30.

17. Ibid., p. 284.
18. Ibid., p. 53.
19. Ibid., p. 46.
20. Saul Bellow, *Herzog* (New York: The Viking Press, 1964), p. 309.
21. Ibid., p. 140.
22. Ibid., p. 19.
23. Ibid., p. 32.
24. Ibid., p. 274.
25. Ibid., pp. 72 and 147, for example.
26. Saul Bellow, *Mr. Sammler's Planet* (New York: Viking Press; London: Weidenfeld and Nicolson, 1970), p. 26.
27. Ibid., p. 235.
28. Ibid., p. 228.
29. Ibid., p. 313.
30. Ibid., p. 237.
31. Saul Bellow, *Humboldt's Gift* (New York: The Viking Press, 1975), p. 460.
32. Ibid., p. 202.
33. Ibid., p. 24.
34. Ibid., p. 414.
35. Ibid., p. 406.
36. Ibid., p. 3.
37. Ibid., p. 218.
38. Ibid., p. 293.
39. Ibid., p. 260.
40. Ibid., p. 396.
41. Ibid., p. 365.
42. Ibid., p. 460.

NOTES TO CHAPTER 8

1. Ken Kesey, *Sometimes a Great Notion* (New York: Bantam Books, 1965), p. 425.
2. Ibid., p. 346.
3. Ibid., p. 12.
4. Ibid., p. 227.

NOTES TO CHAPTER 9

1. Irving Howe, *Decline of the New* (New York: Harcourt, Brace and World, 1970), pp. 110, 97.
2. Richard Poirier, *A World Elsewhere: The Place of Style in American Literature* (New York: Oxford University Press, 1966), p. 16.
3. Nathan A. Scott, Jr., *Modern Literature and the Religious Frontier* (New York: Harper and Brothers, 1958), pp. 66–67.
4. Robert Scholes, *The Fabulators* (New York: Oxford University Press, 1967), pp. 106–7.
5. See Albert D. Van Nostrand, *Everyman His Own Poet: Romantic*

Gospels in American Literature (New York: McGraw-Hill Book Co., 1968), pp. 3–5.

6. On the last of these, language, see Tony Tanner, *City of Words: American Fiction 1950-1970* (New York: Harper and Row, 1971); and Richard Poirier, *The Performing Self: Compositions and Decompositions in the Languages of Contemporary Life* (New York: Oxford University Press, 1971).

7. Lewis Mumford, ed. *Ralph Waldo Emerson: Essays and Journals* (Garden City: Doubleday and Co., 1968), p. 17.

8. Tony Tanner, *The Reign of Wonder* (Cambridge: Cambridge University Press, 1965), p. 45.

9. Jeffrey L. Duncan, *The Power and Form of Emerson's Thought* (Charlottesville: University of Virginia Press, 1973), p. 49.

10. Michael Cowan, *City of the West: Emerson, America and Urban Metaphor* (New Haven: Yale University Press, 1967), pp. 89–112.

11. Kenneth Burke, "I, Eye, Ay—Emerson's Early Essay 'Nature': Thoughts on the Machinery of Transcendence" in Myron Simon and Thornton Parsons, eds., *Transcendence and Its Legacy* (Ann Arbor: The University of Michigan Press, 1966), p. 8.

12. Edgar Allan Poe, *The Works of Edgar Allan Poe*, Vol. VI, ed. Edwin Markham (New York: Funk & Wagnalls, 1904), p. 124.

13. John F. Lynen, *The Design of the Present: Essays on Time and Form in American Literature* (New Haven: Yale University Press, 1969), pp. 215–16.

14. Daniel Hoffman, *Poe, Poe, Poe, Poe, Poe, Poe, Poe* (Garden City: Doubleday and Co., 1973), p. 211.

15. Edward H. Davidson, *Poe: A Critical Study* (Cambridge: Harvard University Press, 1957), p. 230.

16. Edgar Allan Poe, *The Works of Edgar Allan Poe*, Vol. IX, eds. Edmund Stedman and George Woodberry (New York: Charles Scribner's Sons, 1927), p. 26.

17. Henry David Thoreau, *Walden and Civil Disobedience*, ed. Owen Thomas, (New York: W. W. Norton, 1966), pp. 146–47.

18. Ibid., p. 190.

19. Ibid., p. 211.

20. Ibid., p. 212.

21. Stephen Crane, *The Red Badge of Courage: An Annotated Text with Critical Essays*, ed. Sculley Bradley et al., (New York: W. W. Norton, 1962), p. 24.

22. Ibid., p. 30.

23. Ibid., p. 74.

24. Ibid., p. 90.

25. Ibid., p. 25.

26. Vladimir Nabokov, *Phin* (Garden City, N.Y.: Doubleday, 1957), p. 135.

27. See Robert Detweiler, "Games and Play in Modern American Fiction," *Contemporary Literature*, 17, no. 1 (Winter 1976): 44–63.

28. H. Richard Niebuhr, *Radical Monotheism and Western Culture* (New York: Harper and Row, 1970), p. 53.

29. Shubert Ogden, *The Reality of God and Other Essays* (New York: Harper and Row, 1966), p. 21.

30. Shubert Ogden, *Christ Without Myth: A Study Based on the Theology of Rudolf Bultmann* (New York: Harper and Row, 1961), p. 137.

31. Ibid., p. 137.

32. Ibid., p. 153.

33. Shubert Ogden, *The Reality of God*, p. 31.

34. Ibid., p. 25.

35. Ibid., p. 37.

NOTES TO CHAPTER 10

1. Kurt Vonnegut, Jr., *The Sirens of Titan* (New York: Dell Publishing Co., 1972), p. 17.

2. Ibid., p. 32.

3. Ibid., p. 313.

4. Kurt Vonnegut, Jr., *Mother Night* (New York: Avon Books, 1966), p. 136.

5. Kurt Vonnegut, Jr., *God Bless You Mr. Rosewater; or, Pearls Before Swine* (New York: Dell Publishing Co., 1974), p. 7.

6. Ibid., p. 18.

7. Ibid., p. 137.

8. Kurt Vonnegut, Jr., *Slaughterhouse-Five; or, the Children's Crusade: A Duty-Dance With Death* (New York: Delacorte Press, 1969), p. 65.

9. Ibid., pp. 87–88.

10. Kurt Vonnegut, Jr., *Breakfast of Champions; or, Goodbye Blue Monday* (New York: Delacorte Press, 1973), p. 209.

11. Ibid., p. 210.

NOTES TO CHAPTER 11

1. John Barth, *The Floating Opera* (New York: Bantam Books, 1972), p. 49.

2. Ibid., p. 50.

3. Ibid., p. 57.

4. Basil Wiley, *Seventeenth Century Background* (Garden City: Doubleday and Co., 1953), pp. 83–97.

5. John Barth, *The Sot-Weed Factor* (Garden City: Doubleday and Co., 1960), p. 733.

6. Ibid., p. 670.

7. Ibid., p. 140.

8. Ibid., p. 366.

9. Ibid., p. 794.

10. John Barth, *Giles Goat-Boy* (Garden City: Doubleday and Co., 1966), p. 52.

11. Ibid., p. 439.

12. Ibid., p. 575.

13. John Barth, *Lost in the Funhouse* (New York: Bantam Books, 1969), p. 166.

14. John Barth, *Chimera* (New York: Random House, 1972), p. 9.

15. Ibid., p. 17.

16. Ibid., p. 199.

17. Ibid., p. 256.

18. Ibid., p. 291.

19. Ibid., p. 308.

20. John Barth, *Letters* (New York: G. P. Putnam's Sons, 1979), p. 233.

21. Ibid., p. 650.

22. Ibid., p. 341.

NOTES TO CHAPTER 12

1. Thomas Pynchon, *V.* (New York: Bantam Books, 1964), p. 419.

2. Ibid., p. 285.

3. Ibid., p. 297.

4. See Theodore Ziolkowski, *The Novels of Hermann Hesse* (Princeton: Princeton University Press, 1965), pp. 255–261.

5. Thomas Pynchon, *The Crying of Lot-49* (New York: Bantam Books, 1967), p. 13.

6. Ibid., p. 18.

7. Ibid., p. 92.

8. Ibid., p. 61.

9. Ibid., p. 97.

10. Ibid., p. 56.

11. Ibid., p. 137.

12. Ibid., p. 136.

13. Ibid., p. 135.

14. Thomas Pynchon, *Gravity's Rainbow* (New York: Bantam Books, 1974), p. 368.

15. Ibid., p. 842.

16. Ibid., p. 102.

17. Ibid., p. 281.

18. Ibid., p. 726.

19. Ibid., p. 243.

20. Ibid., p. 506.

21. Ibid., p. 317.

22. Ibid., p. 377.

23. Ibid., p. 861.

24. Ibid., p. 192.

25. Ibid., p. 705.

26. Ibid., pp. 102–3.

NOTES TO CONCLUSION

1. The tendency of criticism in dealing with moral and spiritual matters in American literature is to treat them as derived from or as standing in opposition to orthodox Christianity, especially Puritanism. A sampling of studies representative of this approach would be Sacvan Bercovitch, *The Puritan Origins of the American Self* (New Haven: Yale University Press, 1975); John F. Lynen, *The Design of the Present: Essays on Time and Form in American Literature* (New Haven: Yale University Press, 1969); and F. Walter Herbert, Jr., *Moby-Dick and Calvinism* (New Brunswick: Rutgers University Press, 1977). My point about wisdom is that the moral and spiritual concerns of American literature need not be taken as watered-down versions of orthodox Christianity, that such concerns have integrity and sources of their own.

2. See, for example, Glendon E. Bryce, *A Legacy of Wisdom: The Egyptian Contribution to the Wisdom of Israel* (Lewisburg, Pa.: Bucknell University Press, 1979), pp. 148–49.

3. ". . . the wisdom books say nothing whatever about Israel, its history and political vicissitudes, its peculiar status as the people of God, its cult, laws, priesthood or prophets. In these books the center of interest is the individual and his needs, ambitions, and problems; and even when the problems of the relation of the individual to society are discussed it is human society in general rather than the specific community of Israel to which reference is made." R. N. Whybray, *Wisdom in Proverbs: The Concept of Wisdom in Proverbs 1-9* (Naperville, Illinois: Alec R. Allenson, 1965), p. 14.

4. See Richard D. Mosier, *Making the American Mind: Social and Moral Ideas in the McGuffey Readers* (New York: Russell and Russell, 1965), p. 62, and John A. Nietz, *Old Textbooks* (Pittsburgh: University of Pittsburgh Press, 1961), pp. 78–79. Nietz writes, "It has been recognized by students of history that the lessons in the McGuffey *Readers* did much to set the standards of morality and of the social life in the pioneering west for more than half a century" (p. 78). See also Ruth Miller Elson, *Guardians of Tradition: American Schoolbooks of the Nineteenth Century* (Lincoln: University of Nebraska Press, 1964). Nietz's book details the circulation of the readers I have mentioned and described. My judgment that these readers are manuals in wisdom, however, can only be tested by reading them.

5. "They had learned that man has a very close kinship with the world around him, that he is made of the same stuff, that connection with things is important to his health, that in a way, man is a brother to the world around him. He belongs to the earth." Walter Brueggemann, *In Man We Trust: The Neglected Side of Biblical Faith* (Richmond: John Knox Press, 1972), p. 66. Brueggemann calls the court theologians of tenth century Israel "Renaissance Men" (p. 61). Incidentally, Brueggemann's subtitle represents a conclusion from the perspective of the

Notes

church. I would say that wisdom was not neglected by extraecclesiastical religious orientations.

6. A major example of this way of defining religion, a method having certain philosophical roots which I shall not here explicate or defend, is William James's definition in the lecture entitled "Circumscriptions of the Topic" in his *Varieties of Religious Experience* (New York: Collier Macmillan Publishers, 1961).

7. Readers familiar with formalist or structuralist thought will recognize in this treatment of system the influence of Roman Jakobson's theory of the dominant. See his essay, "The Dominant," in Ladislav Matejka and Krystyna Pomorska, eds., *Readings in Russian Poetics: Formalist and Structuralist Views* (Cambridge: M. I. T. Press, 1971), pp. 82–87. He says, for example, "this aspect of formalist analysis in the field of poetic language had a pioneering significance for linguistic research in general, since it provided important impulses toward overcoming and bridging the gap between the diachronic and the synchronic method of chronological cross section" (p. 87).

8. Georg Lukács, *The Theory of the Novel: A Historico-philosophical Essay on the Forms of Great Epic Literature*, trans. Anna Bostock (Cambridge: M. I. T. Press, 1971), p. 88.

9. See William MaKane, *Prophets and Wise Men* (Chatham: SCM Press, 1965), pp. 49–54, and Zvi Adar, *The Biblical Narrative* (Jerusalem: Goldsberg's Press, 1959), especially p. 56.

10. See, for example, Paul Hernadi, *Beyond Genre: New Directions in Literary Classification* (Ithaca: Cornell University Press, 1972), pp. 156ff.; C. L. Sibusiso Nyembezi, *Zulu Proverbs* (Johannesburg: Witwatersrand University Press, 1963), pp. 4–5; Dwight Edwards Marvin, *Curiosities in Proverbs* (New York: G. P. Putnam's Sons, 1916), pp. 67–87; and Archer Taylor, *The Proverb and an Index to the Proverb* (Copenhagen: Rosenkilde and Bagger, 1962), pp. 27, 31.